bodacious womanist wisdom

bodacious womanist wisdom

LINDA H. HOLLIES

THE PILGRIM PRESS CLEVELAND

Dedicated to my personal sages and women of wisdom

Mama, Doretha Robinson Adams, Big Mama, Eunice Robinson Wade, and Granny, Lucinda Robinson Weston, my life sources; Barbara Jean Baker Vinson-Van Buren, my "bestest-sista" friend; Darlene Sims Lee and Elizabeth Clark Brown, my school years' "best friends"; Ms. Ethel Sims, Ms. Catherine Jones, and Aunt Sweetie, neighborhood "mothers"; Thelma Nunn Pryor and Madine Blakley, lifelong church sistas; Hortense House and Della Burt, teacher/mentors and friends; Emma Justes and Emilie Townes, seminary professors and role models; JoClare Wilson and Cynthia Smitko, CPE guides and pushers; Helen Marie Fannings Ammons and Marilyn Magee, "sista-mothers" and friends; Linda Foster Mumson, Barbara Issacs, and Cecelia Long, North Illinois path clearers; Ida Easley, Fran Brandon, and Brenda Heffner, seminary prayer group; Marie Antoinette Carson, great woman, good friend; Vera Jo Edington and Joyce E. Wallace, Twinkling Butterfly Club; Harlene Harden, Beverly J. Garvin, Vanessa Stephens-Lee, Cynthia Belt, LaSandra Dolberry, Deborah Shumake, Carolyn Wilkins, Michelle Cobb, Juana Dunbar, and Carolyn Abrams, who love me unconditionally; Valerie Bridgeman Davis and Geneieve Brown, who were personal prophets in calling me to fly! Daisybelle Thomas Quinney, Oledia Bell, "Sisthurs"; Eleanor L. Miller, my pastor and intercessor; Lucille Brown; Ruby Earven; Ray Margaret Hall, surrogate mothers, sages, and bodacious women of wisdom! And to every clergy sista around the world!

In memory of Rev. Dr. Janet Hopkins and Rev. Constance Wilkerson.

The Pilgrim Press, 700 Prospect Avenue, Cleveland, Ohio 44115-1100
pilgrimpress.com
© 2003 by Linda H. Hollies

Printed in the United States of America on acid-free paper

08   07   06   05   04   03   5   4   3   2   1

Library of Congress Cataloging-in-Publication Data

Hollies, Linda H.
    Bodacious womanist wisdom / Linda H. Hollies.
      p. cm.
    Includes bibliographical references.
    ISBN 0-8298-1529-5 (pbk. : alk. paper)
    1. African American women—Religious life. 2. Womanist
theology. I. Title.

BR563.N4H645   2003
230'.082—dc22

2003055543

CONTENTS

THE MASK

*D*on't be fooled by me! Don't be fooled by the face I wear, for I wear a thousand masks that I'm afraid to take off, and none of them are me. Pretending is an art that is second nature with me, but, don't be fooled. For God's sake, don't be fooled. I give the impression that I'm secure, that all is sunny and unruffled with me, within as well as without; that confidence is my name and coolness is my game; that the water is calm and I'm in command, and that I need no one. But don't believe me. Please!

My surface may be smooth, but my surface is my mask. Underneath lies the real me in confusion, fear, and aloneness. But I hide this. I don't want you to know. I panic at the thought of my weakness and fear being exposed. That is why I frantically create a mask to hide behind: a nonchalant, sophisticated facade to help me pretend, to shield from the glance that knows. But such a glance is precisely my salvation and I know it—that is, if it's followed by acceptance and if it's followed by love. It's the only thing that will assure me of what I cannot assure myself: that I am worth something.

But I don't tell you this—I don't dare! I'm afraid your glance will not be followed by acceptance and love. I'm afraid you'll think less of me, that you'll laugh at me. And your laughter would kill me. I'm afraid that deep down I am nothing, and that you will see this and reject me. So I play my game—my desperate game—a facade of assurance without. Yet there is a trembling child within.

I idly chatter with you in suave tones of surface talk. I tell you everything that is really nothing, and nothing of what is everything: of what's crying inside me. So when I go through my routine, try to listen to what I'm not saying—what I'd like to say, what I need to say, but what I can't say. I don't like hiding. Honestly! I don't like this superficial game I'm playing, this phony game. I'd like to be genuine and spontaneous and ME! But, you've got to help me.

You've got to hold out your hand even when it's the last thing I seem to want. For only you can call me into aliveness. Each time you're kind and gentle, each time you try to understand because you really care, my heart begins to grow wings—very small wings, very feeble wings, but wings. With your sensitivity and power of understanding, you can breathe life into me. I want you to know that. I want you to know how important you are to me, how you can be the creator of the person that is me—if you choose to. Please choose to. You alone can break down the wall behind which I tremble. You alone can release me from my world of loneliness and uncertainty.

Do not pass me by. Please. Do not pass me by. It will not be easy for you. A long conviction of worthlessness builds strong walls. The nearer you approach, the more blindly I will strike back. I fight against the very thing I cry out for. But I'm told that love is stronger than walls. In this lies my hope. Please try to beat down those walls with firm hands, but with gentle hands, for a child is very sensitive.

Who am I? I am someone you know very well. For I am every individual that you meet!

—*Anonymous*

THERE IS A DOCTOR
IN THE HOUSE!

*T*his book is filled with healing roots, herbs, tonics, and potions for what ails us and keeps us from being able to embrace the new, the better, the best that God has in store for us. We need new thoughts, new directions and new attitudes for a new way of living. So, as a doctor, I have prepared my medicine bag with some down-home remedies that Womanist Wisdom dictated in our past. Believe me, I've had to take them all! And they work. You may not like the smell or the taste, but, they bring healing for what ails us.

In this medicinal bag you will find asafetida bags to ward off colds—cold nights, cold feet, and folks with cold, indifferent attitudes. There is turpentine with sugar for the sore throats and sneezing that prevent us from speaking truth to the idiots in our lives. You will find some goose grease and beef tallow for the lingering coughs and chest congestion that come from stuffing a million years of unshed tears. There is some Black Draught and castor oil with orange pop for cleaning out your systems of old toxic relationships that have kept you stuck in "one down" positions.

Granny told me to include some cow-chip tea for your internal strengthening, which provides the ability to "just say no" to both fools and foolishness! There is Watkins Liniment for rubdowns and the growing pains thaat come as we reach out to embrace new ways for new days!

There is a bottle of quinine, one of coal oil, and even the famous Father John's Emulsion, which are preventive medicines that help us to become strong enough not to return to the limiting, confining, and restrictive relationships and behaviors of our yesterdays!

There are bottles of iodine and mercurochrome for every cut and scrape that trifling individuals have placed upon the tablets of our hearts. And last but certainly not least, I brought some paregoric for colic and for the perpetual whiners who keep repeating the same patterns with different men, coming up with the same broken heart.

Sisters, I do declare that there is a doctor in the house! For there is a balm in Gilead! Dr. Jesus has come to cure sin-sick souls and to make the wounded whole. Take as prescribed and then get ready to shake, step, and run into better tomorrows with less drama. I can't proclaim, "No more drama!" But, Girlfriend, I declare you can have less!

Every chapter of *Bodacious Womanist Wisdom* contains a story about a biblical "certain woman" who has learned lessons and offers to teach us if we are willing to learn. Every chapter contains an ancient proverb for us to ponder. For as Solomon gathered the ancient wisdom of the known world, these proverbs taught lessons to the serious students of life. They will teach us again today. The good news is that Wisdom is a woman who knows our life story. She yearns to have us become wise. She is a willing teacher. She watched our formation, as she describes the creation in chapter 8 of Proverbs. She cheered for us then and wants to cheer our good successes now.

Womanist Wisdom is that learned by women of color who have grappled with the issues of race, sex, and class discrimination and yet continue to rise above the odds and the world's expectations. Womanist Wisdom gives you a word of sage knowledge. It's not the "easy" way. But it's the way of courage. At every chapter's end, a bodacious woman dares to tell you what she has had to do in order to learn life's lessons and pass life's tests so that she can preach, teach, and write what she's known to be truth for the journey.

This is a graduate course in womanist theology! It is for those who have matriculated through the lower courses with demonstrated skills and are now ready to add even more knowledge and skill to their backpacks as they move on to higher places in God. I pray that you are ready for the encounter with Womanist Wisdom. The girl does not play. This is not stuff for sissies, whiners, and cry babies! If you are not thick skinned, filled with the scars of previously won battles, and already have some victories in life to lean back on, put this book down!

One of my female associates, Rev. Dr. Jessica Ingram, told me years ago that in order for me to minister to women, as I have been mandated to do, God would always keep my battles fresh so that my testimony would stay current. The girl did not lie. One of my best male friends, Rev. Anthony Earl, told me that when we reach new levels, we must be prepared to face new devils! As we journey to the high places, the enemy puts more seasoned players in our path. The boy did not lie. But the Bible says that "all things work together for the good of those who love God and are called according to God's purpose" (Rom. 8:28). I have placed my life on this scripture and encourage you to do the same.

Once again, it is my tremendous privilege to present to you the biblical life lessons that I have had to experience and "taste test" first. I pray that they help you on your journey. For God is yet calling for bodacious, wise women to go into all the world announcing that Jesus is Lord, to the glory of God. This I know without a doubt! Know that I'm praying for and with you as we do what women have always been called to do!

Author's Note about Scripture

A note about scripture references: I take great personal liberty with scripture! I believe it was written for me. And I know it needs to have inclusive language so none of us are excluded. So I have attempted to be true to documenting the sources of every scriptural reference, using the New International Version for many of them. However, this version is not wholly inclusive in language. Therefore, I pray you will be indulgent as you read your selected version and find it does not say exactly what I have stated. It's what I saw and felt was intended.

Acknowledgments

"How rich and glorious is the portion God offers us . . . How vast are the resources of God's power open to us who have faith."
(Eph. 1:18–19)

How can I acknowledge more of the vast and wonderful network of folk who have touched my life and shared their love, care, prayers, and wise counsel with me? Several pages could not contain their names. An entire book could not hold their gifts to my life. Only eternity will be able to reveal my "rich and glorious portion" of kin, friend, and family. I owe each one named untold gratitude.

A book is never written in isolation. All the persons who touch, influence, inspire and even hinder your life help you in the writing process. The lessons you have learned and the individuals who taught you hover over your shoulders, waiting to see if you mastered the materials. In the same way that "it takes a village to raise a child," it takes your entire life community to write a book.

I'm thankful to my life community for my personal experiences and awareness of the journey of forgiveness. Many are the charitable and gracious souls who have forgiven me when I have stumbled, blundered, and just plain messed up! I have been picked up, lifted up, forgiven, and blessed to grow and to become by my life community.

My family of origin heads this list of folks who helped to write this book. My grandmothers, Lucinda Weston, Eunice Wade, Ethel Kellom, and Lessie Bell King, live in me, speak to me, and continue to admonish and cheer me as they watch from the realms of glory. My Big Daddy, Dock Wade, is with them and I appreciate the loving role modeling he provided. My parents, James and Doretha Adams, gave me life and granted me the necessary lessons, which have taught me to hold on to God's unchanging hand! My aunt, Barbara Weston, taught me, by example, the art of meditation, relaxing, releasing, and letting go of yesterday's pain. My uncle, her spouse, Clenton Weston, taught me how to be there for family. Finally, my father in ministry, Rev. James A. Anderson, opened the doors to professional ministry to me. All of these now await me on the "other side." I simply pray that I teach their lessons of wisdom well. For, truly, they taught me with their lives.

My siblings and extended family are the rich soil that has nurtured my soul. For Jacqui, Bob, and Troy; Riene, Tony, Lynne, Michael, and Missy; Regina, Arthur, Raymond, Ibn, and Millicient; James Jr., Jeanette, Noah, and Mohanna; Eddie, Onnette, Eddie Jr., and Candance; David, Kim, Dave Jr., and Ean, and Robert Tyrone and Lisa, I give God thanks and praise.

Finally, my husband, Mista Chuck, is my soul mate and best friend. My daughter, Grian Eunyke, her sons, Giraud and Gamel, her daughter, Symphony, and my sons, Gregory Raymond and Grelon Renard Everett, have each taught me lessons and learned because of me how to love and to forgive. My "family" is another name for Love! Chuck's children have included me and mine in their family circle over these thirty-plus years and wisdom demands that I name them: Pam and Erin, JoAnne, Paul, Lacie, Cory, and Darian "Bear"; Donna, Ronald Charles, and Anita.

In addition to the children of my womb, there are daughters of my heart: Angie Hooks, Jacqui Ford, Tracy Flaggs, Darlene Webster, and Sandy Adams. There are brothers who have helped me along life's winding road and made my life easier. These are Da Boys, my colleagues, brothers, and friends, and their spouses, who always have my back: Dr. Zawdie K. Abiade (and Nancy), Apostle Anthony Earl (and Rev. Bobbie), Dr. Michael Carson (and Rev. Katherine), Dr. Dennis Robinson (and Rev. Darlene) and Dr. Donald Guest, (and Brenda).

I have some primary cheerleaders who pump me up and call me to write "on demand": Kim Sadler, Linda Peavy, Yvette Moore, Rev. Marge, Phil and Azariah Bermann, and Rev. Cynthia Stewart. I have an awesome beautician who not only hooks up my hair and keeps the gray away but also ministers to me with dazzling homemade quilted wall hangings, Pamela Tardy. And I'm grateful to God for the excellent ministry of my copyeditor, Kristin Firth, who makes my words clearer.

These are the folks who are responsible for me being the bodacious, wise woman that I am today. I have been touched, impacted, and inspired by their lives. For each of them and more, I give God total praise! My prayer is that they, too, are always surrounded by Wisdom's counsel.

Shalom, my sisters, God's best shalom!

—Sista Linda

WHAT IS A WOMANIST?

onsider this actual scene: In a room are three pastors who are peers on the same staff. There sits a white male, a white female who is feminist, and a black woman who is womanist. A controversy has arisen that pits the two females against the male. It's a very familiar scene. The black female had taken the matter to her white female counterpart seeking clarity, options, and support. But when they are together with the white male, the feminist says: "We don't have the luxury of building coalitions in this place. I feel that Linda bringing this issue to me for discussion was inappropriate. I will not take sides simply because we are both women."

Now consider this actual scene: Sitting at lunch are four black womanist pastors from different parts of the country. They are sharing "war stories" and strategies of moving ahead in the church world in spite of the racist and sexist obstacles that continue to obstruct. The woman who has the greatest amount of clout, power, and responsibility in her position talks about the white feminists on her job who are making it extremely difficult for her. She says. "I told the bishop that if I had not come to this position on the backs of thousands of other black women, and if there were not thousands of women of color banking on my success, I'd tell them to take this job and stick it! But since I stand for too many people of color, I shall not be moved!"

In the times in which we live, women of every color and hue are familiar with unequal opportunity. We have grown accustomed to being the last hired, first fired, and least paid. For the glass and stained glass ceiling keeps bumping all of our heads, despite affirmative action, which acted more favorably for white women than for black people! For the options and strategies utilized by the feminist and the womanist are extremely different.

A womanist approaches life with the spirit of wisdom from our foremothers and their sewing circles and quilting bees. A patchwork quilt is a thing of beauty and it's also a utilitarian article offering warmth from exposure to cold. In the days of our foremothers, scraps were saved, stored, and utilized by the women's sewing circles and quilting bees. These circles provided a time for socializing, nurturing, networking, and caring for women who were isolated by distance and lack of phones and easy travel.

A quilting bee was a time of women celebrating women's work. It was a gift of Womanist Wisdom. A scrap became a medium through which a woman would share a story about her life. As the needles darted here and there, thread was exchanged, the pattern was extended, and the lives of several families became interwoven. The lives of the sewing and quilting women were patched together as well. As the women gathered, they forged bonds of sisterhood and spoke into existence the future they would never see.

Both black and white women had sewing circles and quilting bees. Both groups needed the quilted products for use by their families. But the quilting circles became a metaphor for the difference between feminist and womanist. White women could hold their quilting bee when it was convenient for their schedules. It became a time of invitation, to host and make sure the "help" got the house and the food properly prepared before the guests arrived. Black women held their quilting bees after the work hours were completed. They took turns going from shanty to shanty as necessary. Their quilting scraps were often just that, the scraps from the leftovers of the "big house." Never did they have the opportunity to go into town for the luxury of selecting and purchasing the materials out of which they would make clothes that would one day be the patches for quilts. The simple issue of individual preference over and against community need began centuries ago.

The women who worked together, quilting patches into beauty, both affirmed and confirmed the life changes they were forced to endure, and they validated the birthing of new and different selves among themselves. In both the "big house" and in the shanty, these women saved each other's sanity and didn't know it. They kept children from being abused and men from being murdered in their sleep and didn't know it. They encouraged the artistic side of each other and didn't know it. But the sewing circle and the quilting bees, seen as ways of doing "the necessary," was Womanist Wisdom's way of gathering women.

One year I searched the Smithsonian Institute for the quilt mentioned in Alice Walker's *In Search of Our Mother's Gardens*. It was a quilt done in black and white scraps depicting the seven stations of the cross, The artist was simply named as "A Negro Slave." The quilt became her act of self-expression and creativity. It continues to bless our community today.

Without the benefit of sophisticated, technological advances like computers, satellites, or university courses in women's studies and equal rights amendments, these quilting women stroked each other, encouraged each other, pushed each other, and demanded that the life presented to them be one of dignity, honor, self-fulfillment, quality relationships, and the ability to be heard in this "circle of sisters." They sewed without judgment or criticism. They quilted without jealousy and snide rebukes. They varied in skill levels, yet together they created a quilt that would be used. Whatever the circumstances and the vantage points of the quilting women, Womanist Wisdom allowed us this precious time and space to establish the way we approach the struggle to become whole.

"In the black community, the aggregate of the qualities which determine . . . the uprightness of character and soundness…must always take into account the circumstances, the paradoxes and the dilemmas that constrict blacks to the lowest range of self-determination. Forced to the lowest rungs of the social, political and economic hierarchy, black existence is deliberately and openly controlled. The vast majority of blacks suffer every conceivable form of denigration. Their lives are named, defined and circumscribed by whites."[1] When another group even determines what pieces you will use to patch together your "quilt," it gives the event new new meaning and us as quilters new awareness of our sameness and our differences.

At the quilting bee in the "big house," there was an exchange of information. Whether or not it was interpreted as "girl talk," gossip, or news of new arrivals and departures in the area, it was simply conversation. Whether the talk centered around the way in which decent help was hard to find or how the house and its new decorations were appealing and trendy, it was not always life changing. If the situation focused on relationships of courtship, marriage, family ties, or even divorce, there was a thread of connection that tied generations, traditions, and history. The quilt was made. Souls were encouraged. Hearts were uplifted. Laughter could be heard.

At the quilting bee down in the slave quarters or in the shanty, the talk was of survival. Mere existence and daily struggle did not make for light-hearted banter and chit-chat. The wisdom from the community sages, the "word" heard by "invisible" help and news of who had been sold, bought, bartered away, or murdered was whispered as counsel. The slave quilters taught each other how to survive and to endure. They counseled those whose families had been torn apart, children sold, and significant other taken to places unknown. They validated their painful realities, prayed for strength, and promised to keep watch for the children and loved ones left behind, if and when something should happen to them. Life was never usual. Friendships were never forever. Hearts were always burdened. Souls were seldom encouraged. Yet the quilt was made. Pastoral care was provided. Life went on, for Womanist Wisdom had gathered the women.

"As a black, she has had to endure all the horrors of slavery and living in a racist society; as a worker, she has been the object of continual exploitation, occupying the lowest place on the wage scale and restricted to the most demeaning and uncreative jobs; as a woman she has seen her physical image defamed and been the object of the white master's uncontrollable lust and subjected to all the ideals of white womanhood as a model to which she should aspire; as a mother she has seen her children torn from her breast and sold into slavery, she has seen them left at home, without affection or attention, while she was forced to attend to the needs of the offspring of the ruling class."[2] And, in this very real world of painful existence, black women built coalitions in quilting bees that helped to hold community together and put patches on wounded and bleeding souls.

The counsel of survival was essential. The sages of the remaining community were forced to share the secrets, pass on the knowledge and leave behind the snippets of information that would be the thread that knitted an abandoned people together. Womanist is another word for pastor, caregiver, and womb of being. Womanist is coalition. Womanist is building, gathering, and bridge-building for yesterday, today, and tomorrow. The quilt scraps might be hand-me-downs but the quilt does the job of providing warmth and protection. The quilt becomes the vehicle for the "approved" gathering of black, female, "nonpersons." Womanist is another word for diligent worker and preserver of black life. Womanist is another name for community love and concern.

The quilting bees continue. In black communities across the country we continue sharing the counsel of survival, in both formal and informal structures. The care of the entire community is our concern. Without being voted into elected leadership or being provided with stipends for the many hours of work involved, the patching of "achy-breaky" hearts, the mending of wounded spirits, and the stitching of broken promises call black women together for the making of the womanist quilt.

Womanist Wisdom is acutely aware that "racism is the domination of a people which is justified by the dominate group on the basis of racial distinctions. It is not only individual acts, but a collective institutionalized activity. It is the consensus of private persons that gives racism its derivative power."[3] The isolationist stance of white feminism cannot presume to understand this black community ethos and necessity. Womanist theology stems from the biblical mandate of the oppressed group being delivered and moving into freedom.

Coalition among women of color is notable in the Moses narrative in chapters 1 and 2 of the book of Exodus. Shiphrah and Puah were midwives who refused to cooperate with the Pharaoh's plan for wholesale slaughter of every male infant born to the Hebrew community. The political structure worked against their individual defiance. But Womanist Wisdom provided coalition whereby these two women gave their "piece" to the quilt of community need. They were "community mothers" who actively engaged in the counsel of survival.

Having the same womanist mind-set, the biological mother of Moses, Jocabed, and her daughter, Miriam, joined this unofficial coalition and further stitched the quilt for the Hebrew community's deliverer to survive, grow, and thrive in the midst of hostile and foreign territory. As a "sister mother," Miriam, hearing the sage counsel being whispered throughout the women's gatherings, was able to secure permission of Moses' adoptive mother to have him nurtured through infancy by his own biological mother in his own home and threatened community.

Deliverance for the minority community, God's chosen people, was possible due to women of color being filled with Womanist Wisdom. With passive resistance they refused to cooperate with the male power structure. Utilizing the "scraps" available to them, these women gathered to quilt a covering of freedom. Their acts of coalition blessed their community. Their acts of pastoral care for each other blessed them, individually and collectively. Scripture details that "Because the midwives feared God, God gave them families of their own" (Ex. 1:21).

The care and welfare of the whole community is biblically centered for the womanist. "The understanding of God as Creator, Sustainer, Comforter and Liberator, took on life as black women agonized over their own pain, and celebrated the hope that as God delivered the Israelites, they would be delivered as well. The God of the Old and New Testaments became real in the consciousness of oppressed black women. Though they were politically impotent, they were able to appropriate certain themes of the Bible which spoke to their reality."[4]

The individualized stance of white feminism is a power-based understanding. The man they call "father" is powerful, because of the color of his skin and ancestry. They man they choose to have a personal and intimate relationship with is powerful. The men they call son, brother, uncle, or cousin are powerful for the same reasons. The power stems from the dominant group to which they belong, not the wealth or influence they have accumulated. This dominant, decision-making group of men are the power brokers, enforcers, and keepers of the laws, courts, and economics that affect us all. Through blood ties the white feminist inherits the benefits of power and can afford to back away from issues not directly of concern to her. The quilt of her familial heritage is a strong covering indeed.

Dr. Martin Luther King Jr. best summed up the pain incurred when the womanist expects support from her feminist sister and finds herself standing alone. In his book *Where Do We Go from Here?* he states, "It is not enough to say, 'We love the Negroes, we have many Negro friends.' White liberals must demand justice for Negroes. Love that does not satisfy justice is no love at all. It is merely sentimental affection, little more than what one would feel for a pet. . . . Power without love is reckless and abusive. . . . Love without power is sentimental and anemic. Power at its best is love implementing the demands of justice. Justice at its best is love correcting everything that stands against love."[5]

For the womanist, "love correcting everything" is a quilt that covers sexism and racism, as well as all the other "isms" that enslave a community. A love that corrects everything demands that the quilting bees that hand down the counsel of survival continue and spread. Store bought coverings, mail order blankets, and foreign-made, cheap bed throws are plentiful. But the womanist knows that an authentic, hand-stitched, pattern-cut, and community-pieced quilt is yet in great demand. And it's extremely costly.

A handmade quilt is a rare commodity in the period in which we live. Those of us who yet have them as family heirlooms treasure them and don't regard them lightly or use them as everyday items. Many old quilts, handed down through generations, are used as wall hangings and hung in prominent places for everyone to admire. When you view the finished product, with its delicate stitching, artistic pattern, and smooth edges, it is not the thread knots on the underside that become the topic of conversation, but rather the number of hours and the obvious loving commitment of the quilters.

I am blessed to have friends who quilt. My beautician, Pamela Tardy, has made me two quilts. One hangs in our home, a colorful tapestry of African prints. The other hangs in my office at WomanSpace, an awesome pattern of brown and gold colors. Both of them were Christmas gifts filled with loving prayers. She is wise enough to know that the gift of a quilt is a joy forever. Two former congregation members, Robin Hiezleman and Nicole Proctor, got together and hand stitched me a purple quilt of butterflies as a going-away present. This quilt covers women who come into WomanSpace seeking sanctuary and needing a covering of love. The wisdom of the quilters continues today and for this I'm grateful.

So many black slaves quilted the stations of the cross in order that today's womanist women might have directions pointing to liberation. So many black women kept the scraps and carefully cut and preserved the necessary pieces for our quilt of freedom that warms us today. The womanist legacy of gathering the women in order to share the counsel of survival and to quilt the covering of freedom and equality is a gift to us from Womanist Wisdom. It is still very true that "all of God's chillun needs a covering." Womanist theology recognizes that the only sufficient covering is one big enough, wide enough, and secure enough to cover everything and everybody. This is our continuing mandate. Regardless of the fact that scraps, pieces, and hand-me-downs continue to be the fabric of our quilting in this country, quilt we will. For womanist is to feminist as a patchwork is to a quilt!

WOMAN WISDOM SPEAKS: "How long will you simple ones love simplicity? For scorners delight in their scorning, and fools hate knowledge. Turn at my rebuke; surely I will pour out my spirit upon you; I will make my words known to you" (Prov. 1:22–23).

WOMANIST WISDOM SAYS: It has been the bodacious actions of many foremothers who dared to create a quilt of love for our race and local communities. Their work and service deserve to be noted and applauded. The time has come for us to be the quilters! We can no longer depend upon what has been done in the past. The future is hurrying our way. All of us are called to add our piece to a new quilt. I have one of my grandfather's sister's quilts. I thought that putting it away would preserve it, but the aged pieces are beginning to rot! It's too delicate now to use and needs to be encased in plastic for preservation. It's time for a new handmade quilt!

A BODACIOUS WOMAN will make it her business to begin the collection of pieces that she wants to add to the community quilt of life. She will ensure that the pieces are authentic to the way she has lived her life and wants her story to be told in the days to come. What are the colors that will remind the world of you? What symbols will you use to let them hear you speak? What is the authentic message that you want your pieces to convey? The pieces are being made with the way we live our daily lives. A story will be told about us. Will it really be the story you want to have told?

1

SISTER MAGI

Genesis 38, Matthew 2

*O*f course there were women Magi! What has ever happened in the realm of God without the presence of women? The names of women have been erased. The voices of women have been silenced. The deeds of women have been minimized. But the exploits of women cannot be overlooked, forgotten, or concealed forever! It does appear that what is covered up, neglected, and denied has a way of coming forth with greater force and stronger power. So it's time to uncover, recover, and discover the gifts that women brought to the birth of Jesus!

Had it not been for women, the lineage of Jesus would have been stopped even before the people of Israel were taken captive to Egypt. Genesis 38 records the story of Judah, head of the tribe through which Jesus was born. He had three sons, Er, Onan, and Shelah. Judah took a wife for his oldest son, Er, by the name of Tamar. But Er was not interested in fathering a child to continue the lineage. God killed him. Tamar was married to the next brother, Onan, as was the custom of the day. But this son also followed the fate of his older brother. Judah refused to marry his last son to Tamar and sent her back to her father's house until his son "became of age," so he said.

Tamar waited. And she waited. Finally Womanist Wisdom helped her to see that the last son was being "saved" from death by his father. So Sister Tamar took matters into her own hands. She knew her role as child bearer for the nation. She set herself up outside the city gates as a prostitute, knowing that Judah would be passing that way. He stopped and solicited her wares. She took several articles of his as "payment" for her services. In due time it became known that "Lil' Sister" was pregnant. She was called a harlot. Stoning was to be her lot.

However, she sent the articles she was holding to the head of the tribe. Not only did Judah recognize and acknowledge them, but he is recorded as saying, "She is more right than I, since I did not give her to my son Shelah. And he did not lie with her again" (Gen.38: 26). The twins she bore kept the lineage going so that the Lion of the tribe of Judah, Jesus, could be born!

So when the Son of God is to be born to a young, naive, single virgin girl named Mary, it surely makes perfect sense to me that Womanist Wisdom would be present in the everyday lives and roles of women. When the male Magi appeared, know that the sisters were among them. It's not surprising that their names are not recorded. It's no new thing that what they brought as gifts is not detailed for posterity. I don't find it disturbing that there is no mention of them in the canon of Holy Scriptures. But I know they were there! For Mary needed counsel. Mary needed advice. Mary needed support. And Womanist Wisdom never fails.

Remember that Mary and all other woman in scripture are women of color. There is a cultural memory that we possess. There is a cultural way of doing "woman things." There is a cultural ethos that surrounds our actions regardless of where we are in the world. For it's never been easy to be a woman of color in this world. Every woman is familiar with stress, frustration, worry, obsession, repression, oppression, and dismissal. We have all been on a first-name basis with insecurity, poverty, rip-offs, and turn-offs. We are equal opportunity partners with systematic exclusion, even within the religious structures. But with the guidance of Womanist Wisdom, a gift from God, we pick ourselves up, dust ourselves off, and patch together our lives with other searching, seeking women. And we advance the struggle for liberty and justice for all.

It's been the role of Womanist Wisdom to gather the women. For whether it was in the next tent or next door, down the road or even under our watchful eyes, aggression, violence, crime, murder, rape, robbery, incest, conflict, brutality, and other unnamed evils have made themselves at home in our collective lives. We have had to push past the rejection, separation, death, suicide, murder, domestic violence, divorce, and male disappearance. It makes no difference what country, what ethnic group or tribe, women do hand-to-hand combat with materialism, consumerism, elitism, classism, and sexism. And women of color have always had to contend with the evil of racism. Yet, despite manipulation, exploitation, and downright lies being told about women in the textbooks, the media, and with oral history, we continue to patch our lives together, expand our potential, dream possible dreams, and achieve exploits because Womanist Wisdom is on our side.

The Magi were on a long and tedious journey, following the star. For years they had studied. For years they had dreamed. For years they had planned the trip of their lives. This was the journey that introduced the Son of God to the whole, wide world! This was the journey that would carry news of a Divine Potentate back to the known regions of the inhabited earth. The Magi traveled for many miles, which meant years. They needed a host of supplies, food, and water. They needed animals and animal tenders. They needed those with expertise in pitching tents and making all things ready. They needed cooks. They needed diversion from their difficult days. So, they needed women! Did you really think they would travel without women?

We have always been in the plan of the Almighty. It makes no difference what version of the creation story you hold dear, the first, the second, or Womanist Wisdom's version, women were in the mind of God. Even when Sister Eve chose to do the wrong thing and disobey, God gave her a promise that it would be a child of her womb who would redeem all of humankind. Woman was made to suffer because of Adam and Eve's choice. Woman was made the carrier of nations, the consolation of every race, the strong force in each community, and the persuasion behind political changes. Woman was made the conveyer of both hope and help. Despite her sin, in spite of the condition in which she found herself, regardless of Adam's finger of blame, God had a plan for woman in the redemption story.

Women learned to be seen and not heard. Women learned to learn and be silent. Women learned to see and not see. Women learned to be invisible, to pick up information, to share necessary details, and to transmit values. So, as the Magi studied and researched, the women learned. As the Magi planned, the women prepared. As the Magi worked in the laboratory watching starlit skies, the women worked in the kitchen, talked in the woman's quarters, and shared what was going to happen. As the Magi discussed the gifts needed for a male king, the women considered what his mother would need. For Womanist Wisdom will gather the women, who then help each other survive.

God is our help in ages past, who created us in the image of Divine Intelligence, breathed into us the breath of life, and mandated, dictated, and impelled us to go forth into abundant living. Even though "the world" has denied us proper respect, authentic admiration, and equal dignity, we have been gifted with Womanist Wisdom to see us through. From the earliest recorded history we find women who have been overworked, underpaid, humiliated, used, abused, neglected, and ignored. We have been hurt and we have been made angry. Yet we are sensitive to each others' needs. For we know the story inwardly: "There, but for the grace of God, go I". So, Womanist Wisdom has been at work in the deep recesses of our souls, nurturing, lifting, and admonishing us to look upward and to move ahead. She has worked through our submission, our bitterness, our religious rationalizing, and the clever mental games we play to keep us from facing our own bitter reality. For we have survived. And often we have thrived!

The Magi made the trip from the East. The women were on the journey. They came to view and affirm the tiny King of Kings. The women came to take a peek and to join Mary in the place of women. They met in the fields and embraced. They met over the campfires and shared the wisdom of women of color. They washed eating utensils and the swaddling cloths used for diapers and fed each others' spirits and souls. The Magi brought gold, frankincense, and myrrh. The women brought Mary cloth for new clothes, spices for her meal preparations, and friendship breads from the yeast they had carried over the miles. The Magi talked to Joseph and the shepherds. The women affirmed the innkeeper's wife and the midwife who had assisted Mary. The Magi were the talk of the little community and then of the known world. The women were dismissed as insignificant and disappeared from the records of history. But they were there. Womanist Wisdom made it her business to have them there. Mary needed company. Mary needed a network of support before she and Joseph began another trek, as refugees to Africa to establish another home, this time with an infant named Jesus.

Thank God for the Magi. Thank God for the women, sister Magi, who were with them! Thank God for bodacious Womanist Wisdom, always on the case!

WOMAN WISDOM SPEAKS: "God possessed me at the beginning of the world, before the creation of the world. I have been established from everlasting, from the beginning, before there was ever an earth" (Prov. 8:22–23).

WOMANIST WISDOM SAYS: When a woman's name made it to the books of the Bible, you can best believe that she was more than bodacious! With over 2,500 names in the Bible and women being named less than one third of this total, it says that a "named" sister was filled with wisdom. And of course we have to remember those "certain women" whose wisdom and knowledge are applicable to each and every one of us. We need to go back and take a long, slow look at the women's stories that made it to the genealogy of Jesus Christ. For their stories are ours! We too are in his blood line! Get their wisdom and put it into action in your own life!

A BODACIOUS WOMAN would seek the wisdom of an elder sister. She would take a senior woman that she respects out to lunch and ask her to become a mentor. She would talk with her and stay in touch with her, adopt her and seek her wisdom in matters of the heart and the spirit. For my Granny "usta" say that "bought wisdom is the most expensive!" This means that there are some things we don't have to buy with our lives. We can get the benefits of what an older woman has already done and come through. I have three different "mother-mentors" in my life. They come from three different denominations. They have different levels of life experiences, professional experiences, and church experiences. They have different levels of sophistication. I learn from each of them. I trust their words of wisdom. They all keep me in prayer and in line with words of counsel! Older, seasoned women have already, "been there, done that!" and they are not in competition with us. Find yourself at least one!

2

REINVENTING THE WOMAN!

2 Samuel 20:14–22

*T*here is a book on the market, written by a sista whose name is Patty Rice. It is a fiction, a made-up tale. It is not any single woman's autobiography. It's a combination of all our collective stories. It is a common story about a woman being abused, misused, rejected, abandoned, and kicked to the curb. It is the continuing story of women who are physically, sexually, emotionally, and spiritually raped, time after time. And they always wonder, "What did I do to deserve this?" This book is a work about domestic violence. It's a wonderful example of a woman who discovers her own wisdom. The name of Patty's book is *Reinventing the Woman.*

This book you're reading right now is also for just this particular reason: God is ready to help us reinvent ourselves. Our mandate is to become better than what we currently are. God is tired of our whining, crying, lamenting, and complaining about being victims. The time is over for the "poor me," "look at what they've done to me," "everybody done me wrong" theme song that we love to sing.

We are in a state of war. There is war and there are rumors of war all over the world. There is war in our nation. There is war within our local congregations. There is war in our communities. There is war between sisters. There is war within our homes. And, yes, the average one of us is dealing with an inner war that has us living on the edge.

It is no secret that on September 11, 2001, terrorists brought down three brick and mortar buildings that represented America's military and economic world power; but the reality is that black folk have been at war way before that date. We want to talk about the devastation at Ground Zero. But I invite you to come walk with me through too many black neighborhoods in any urban city within America.

You want to talk about thousands of American casualties? Let's call the roll of black youth murdered in drive-by shootings, killed by white police, taken out by drugs, and rotting to death behind the newest slavery system—prison walls.

If you want to talk about the decline of the DOW and NASDAQ after September 11, let's see if we can number the people of color who were affected when airport skycaps stopped, restaurant kitchens closed, marking rooms shut down, and housekeepers and janitors were told to stay home for three weeks. Most of us are only two paychecks away from bankruptcy in the first place. For in America, the land of the free and home of the slave, we have been and continue to be the last hired and first fired. The war didn't just break out in black America.

Yet, in this time of terrorism and war, in the period of fear and confusion, in this space where the name of God is being called and prayers are being prayed in Congress, the White House, and local schools, God has a significant role for bodacious wise women to play. God has a strategic plan for each one of us to enact. God has an established method of pushing women to the forefront. The time is now. It's time to reinvent the role of women who will work with God.

This is not the time for us to be bickering and backstabbing. This is not the time for us to be catty and small minded. This is not the time for us to stand back and see each other fall and fail. This is not the time to run off and forsake each other. This is not the time to be so concerned about me and mine that all of us are consumed. God is calling us to stop doing business as usual. God is calling us to grow up, stop behaving like little girls, and become the bodacious wise women of God.

God's women are shrewd. God's women are compassionate. God's women are community minded. God's women are miracle workers. God's women are creative. God's women are filled with peace that surpasses understanding. God's bodacious wise women are faithful and stick to their word. God's bodacious wise women are committed. God's bodacious women are wise, especially in times of war.

It's time for reinvention. It's time for a makeover. It's time to come out of the closet. It's time to step up to the plate. It's time to let the world see Jesus in our life. It's time to let them see how we imitate God. God's wisdom formed the world. God's mouth spoke the universe into existence. And God's love called you and me to participate in the act of keeping the mission and the ministry of Jesus alive in the midst of wars and rumors of war.

It's not about the biggest church. It's not about the baddest car. It's not about the sharpest St. John's knit or Ferragamo shoes. It's not about who gets the most engagements. It's not about who commands the highest fees. It's not about who can pull the largest number of silly, emotional, "ain't about nothing, ain't gonna do nothing" sisters together. Friends, it's all about who is the most bodacious wise woman who can discern what's going on around her. It's about the sage who knows, remembers, and has learned from her ancestors. It's about the woman who says what she means and means what she says. It's about the woman whose wisdom is sought. It's about the woman whom the community recognizes has a vital and meaning- ful relationship with God.

I wish I could really teach you all about the life of David. I'd like to have time to personally introduce you to 1 Samuel 25 and all the wise women whom God used in the Davidic reign. I'd like to share with you the life of Abigail, a woman who married a rich but nasty man, Nabal, and stayed there until God make her David's wife, a queen, due to her skills in conflict resolution. I'd love to teach about

Bathsheba, who was raped by David and who lost her husband, Uriah, and her firstborn son. I'd like to help you understand how she hummed to keep her sanity and watched her son Solomon ascend to David's throne.

It would be my pleasure to walk you through the history of Michal, the daughter of Saul and wife of David whose bitterness drove her into both childlessness and isolation. For sure, I'd like to stop by Ms. Tamar's house in 2 Samuel 13, and have you revisit the story of her rape. You'd think this was enough, but her decision to remain in a place of desolation is a sermon all by itself.

There needs to be time for us to share the life of Rizpah in 2 Samuel 21. She was certainly a role model of community ministry. For five months girlfriend waved away the vultures who wanted to eat the dead bones of her sons.

But time! Limited pages! Space and time! Time, space, and limited pages of this book will only allow me to offer you an exegetical exposition of an unnamed woman found in chapter 20 of 2 Samuel. David is fighting to hold his realm together after the coup of his son, Absalom, who had raped Tamar and caused the death of their brother, Ammon. With all the turmoil and terror in the nation and within his family, David finds himself between a rock and a hard place.

In chapter 19, Joab, the captain of the army and nephew of David, comes along while David is having a crying pity party and says, "You are a national disgrace! Stop whining and sniffling over someone who meant you absolutely no good" (2 Sam. 19:1–8). This is a message all by itself to many of us! When David pulled himself together, the folks returned. When we get ourselves together, the right folk will show up. We need to hear what the Holy Spirit is saying to the Church.

The fight between Israel and Judah continued. Revolts, revolutions and uprising continued. The terrorist attacks were fierce. They did strike-and-run violence. A man named Sheba was David's Osama bin Laden. He led Israel in revolt. The first three verses of chapter 20 tell of David's time of abstinence, which is the evidence of what real war does to even macho men. For war took David's sex drive.

Sheba, like bin Laden, ran into a city of refuge. When God had Moses divide the land of Canaan between the twelve tribes of Israel, six cities were to be designated as cities of refuge. The Levites were given the serious responsibility of judging whether persons with blood on their hands would live or die. This was not the role of the priest, but of the psalmists. For nobody escapes responsibility with God.

In a day when an eye for an eye was the norm, God wanted to temper the Law with divine mercy. In Numbers 35:24, God told Moses that the assembly of Levites must judge between the one fleeing and the one seeking revenge. It was the custom. It was the practice. It was the culture. So Sheba fled inside the city gates. In 2 Samuel 20:14–22 the action begins to take place. For Joab knew where Sheba was.

He was ready to act on behalf of King David and began to lay seige to the city. His soldiers were battering the wall to bring it down. But in doing so Joab was about to seal his own fate with the Most High God. For Numbers 35:29, reads "A city of refuge is a legal requirement for Israel throughout the generations to come, wherever you live. Verse 33 states "Do not pollute the land. Do not defile the land where you live and where I dwell, for I, the Lord, dwell among you." We cannot promote war. The church is a city of refuge. You and I are sacred cities, established to save lives.

Joab was about to defile the city of refuge. Then in verse 16, "A wise woman spoke . . ." The words and actions of this wise woman saved many lives. Because of her wisdom, Joab did not ransack the city. "A wise woman spoke . . ." I like this because the Bible calls Wisdom a woman. In Proverbs 1:20–21, Solomon establishes that Wisdom is a female. In Proverbs 8:22, Woman Wisdom speaks for herself.

We don't often hear about wise women in scripture. We know about wise male leaders, like Joseph, Moses, Joshua, David, Solomon, and Stephen, the apostle. We hear about Bezalel, the wise artist who supervised the construction of the first tabernacle. (Ex. 31:1–5) We know that Abigail is called a wise wife, Daniel is called a wise counselor, the Magi, are called wise learners, and Paul is called a wise messenger. But here in the midst of war and terror, we find a wise woman—a bodacious wise woman who reinvents her place in ministry.

This passage is so obscure. This passage is so tucked away in scripture. This passage is another one about an unnamed woman. She has no real identity. We don't get to know her story. We don't have any context to place her in to see how she lived on a daily basis. She is so hidden that I'd overlooked her. My baby sister, Regina C. Pleasant, introduced her to me by asking me a question about her! She was getting ready to preach about her and wanted more insight. I couldn't help her. But I'm so glad she brought this bodacious wise woman into my life! For this nameless woman has much wisdom to offer to women seeking more of God.

Wisdom is a gift from God and it's combined with an energetic search for knowledge of truth. Wisdom's starting point is with God. Any of us who lack wisdom only have to ask God for revelation, knowledge, and understanding. Wisdom is hidden from the foolish, the disobedient, and the rebellious. You cannot drift into wisdom. You cannot purchase wisdom. You cannot coast along and happen to bump up against wisdom. But wisdom comes with a life of serious devotion to God and a continued searching after and longing for more of the mind of God.

"A wise woman spoke." This woman recognized her ability to speak to power with power. This woman's aim was to preserve her community. This woman's accomplishments in the past made others ready to listen to her counsel. She was a woman of action, not just talk. She didn't allow customs, traditions, or cultural limits to abort her role of spokeswoman for God. She accepted her role as a wise woman with a sense of "I can do this!" She had both power and purpose. She wasn't hiding in the spots relegated to women. No, she was among the warriors, part of the Levitical assembly at the gate.

This wise woman became a heroine. It's obvious she had a habit of taking charge . . . "Listen. Listen. I have something to say." She did not hesitate to be outstanding, vocal, and uncompromising. She pushed past the hurts of womanhood and hurried to do what only she could do. This woman waited to be used at the wall surrounding her city.

Walls have always been part of God's story in the earth. Walls fence in and walls lock out. We can easily be on one side of the wall and find ourselves on the wrong side. We, too, have a history of erecting walls. We have become gatekeepers. We have been kept on the other side of the Old Boys Club walls for so long that now we find ourselves better than they are at erecting them against each other.

Walls are a reality. Expect them. Walls are part of the story. Anticipate them. Walls are everywhere. Look for ways to either batter them down, move around them, or crawl over or under them. Or do like this wise woman and make your voice so strong, so powerful that they will listen to you on the other side of the wall.

This means that we have to engage in the war. We can't sit on the sidelines. We will get injured. We will get hurt. We will be wounded. But we are warriors. We can't fight from behind the protected pulpit. We have to enter the battle and lead from the front. We have already been warned, "Many are the afflictions of the righteous, but God delivers them from them all" (Ps. 34:19).

The Dahomey women in Africa were warriors. They refused to let anything get in their way of winning. If one were right-handed, she would cut off their right breast. They refused to let any hindrance cause victory for the other side. When we determine ourselves to fight the good fight of faith, God will make a way somehow. But we have to keep going to the wall.

"A wise woman spoke." Our words have the power of both life and influence. We have to be careful with our words because the proverbs have declared that we are snared, trapped, limited, and devoured by the very words that we speak. God created the earth with only the power of words, and in our tongues we hold the ability to either build or destroy our world. Be careful with your words so that when you speak, folks are listening to wisdom that does not come from your human existence, but from your association with the Wisdom of the Ages, whom we call God.

There is work that only women can do. It's time for us to get busy. We were given worth before there were prophets and apostles. We were given worth before bishops and overseers came on the scene. In the Garden of Eden, God gave woman the prophecy that it would be her seed that would bring forth redemption for the world. God chose a woman to bear the Seed of Life. God had that Seed of Life confess his Messiahship to a dismissed woman by the side of an old well in Samaria. When that Seed was placed upon an old rugged cross, there were three women and only one man at the scene of the crime. It is recorded that there were only four women on their way to do ministry to a dead corpse the day after his death. And there was only one crying woman standing in the dark in a graveyard who got the message directly from that Risen Seed. The message was to go and tell those scared little brothers that Christ had risen from the grave. This is the work assigned to our hands. This is the work that only women can do.

Exalt in your worthiness. Give God thanks and praise for being a woman of worth. And speak worthy messages to all who will lend an ear. "Listen. Listen. I have something to say." Then let your own works and your worthy words praise you in the gates!

WOMAN WISDOM SPEAKS: "Death and life are in the power of the tongue, and those who love it will eat its fruit" (Prov. 18:21).

WOMANIST WISDOM SAYS: Be careful with your words. The Bible instructs us to let our words be few and seasoned with grace. A woman of a few, soft-spoken words is carefully listened to regardless of the wisdom of her words. People have to strain to hear what she says. When you really want attention from someone, lower your voice several decibels. Watch the reactions.

A BODACIOUS WOMAN would do like President Roosevelt and talk softly and carry a big stick. In other words, her actions speak louder than her words. This woman of wisdom called to the army captain and said, "Listen. Listen." When she spoke she told him that she had a plan of action, and she carried it out. A man's head on a platter speaks real loud! We talk too much. We give away too much information. We brag too much. And we don't do half of what we promise or threaten! It's time to change our natural inclinations if we want to be bodacious and wise!

3

STRATEGIES FOR EFFECTIVE CHANGE

Deuteronomy 1:1–11

*M*y schedule was all jazzed up. I felt like a little puppy chasing a stubby tail! I was going around in circles. The month began with us moving into a new house on Friday. My sisters came to help me unpack on Saturday. Early Saturday morning I was on the road for an out-of-town preaching engagement. Monday I left for the Bahamas and the Black United Methodist Clergywomen's Annual Business Meeting. We got back to the states on Friday and I flew into Indianapolis to do a women's retreat for my friend Dr. Elaine Walters.

I got to the hotel at 7:00 in the evening and was preaching before 9:00 P.M. At 5:00 the next morning, I was up preparing the message for the 8:00 A.M. worship. Elaine and I left for the airport at lunchtime because my flight home was scheduled for 1:30 in the afternoon. It was to be a direct flight into Grand Rapids.

I hadn't had a decent meal for almost a day and a half. Lunch was in order. We stopped at a Wendy's because the time frame was so tight. There we made our first mistake. Driving someone else's car, we decided to eat in rather than have carryout. We sat there eating spicy chicken sandwiches too long. We pulled up at the airport with five minutes until departure. Although the skycap was willing to put my luggage on a cart and we ran through the airport like one of the old O. J. Simpson commercials, the plane had pulled away from the gate when we arrived. It was that airline's last flight to my destination—home!

The woman at the counter checked her computer and discovered what airline had another flight that would get me home; however, that spicy chicken sandwich was the most costly we've ever eaten, for it was an additional $303 and required a layover in Chicago. I needed to get home. I was due in another city to preach on Sunday! There was a two-hour wait in that airport and another hour wait in Chicago. When I arrived in Chicago I had to change planes. I went to the scheduled gate area, sat down to read, and fell asleep.

When I awoke, that plane had departed! I missed two planes in one day! I was angry. I was embarrassed to call Chuck again. I felt foolish. I was in the airport both times where planes arrived and departed. I had a ticket to my destination. But I had not managed the necessary changes to get me to my final destination in a decent time frame. Exhaustion had caught up with me. Sleep had slipped up on me. So I blew two opportunities for making the effective moves that could have gotten me home in a timely and direct manner.

I understood the lesson of how the people of God, freed from slavery in Egypt, traveling a direct route that should have taken eleven days, kept going around in circles for forty years and eleven months! They couldn't get with God's strategies for effective change. Their own "stuff" kept getting in the way. Instead of taking God's direct route, they kept themselves in perpetual "layover." Deuteronomy 1:2 records, that it takes eleven days to go from Horeb to Kadesh Barnea by the Mount Seir road. Verses 3–6 say that in the fortieth year, on the eleventh month, Moses proclaimed, "The Lord our God said to us at Horeb, 'You have stayed long enough at this mountain. Break camp and advance . . .'"

Not only would the people have made the required trip as they moved from enslavement to freedom in the promised land, God made them another promise in verse 11 trying to persuade them to move. "May the Lord . . . increase you a thousand times and bless you as promised." If they would only advance, not only would they arrive at their destination, but a thousand-time blessing awaited them! They remained, in the same holding pattern, stuck on stupid. Verse 26 records, "You were unwilling to go up, you rebelled against the commands . . . you grumbled . . . you questioned, 'Where can we go? The people there are stronger and taller . . .'" It doesn't make good sense. The Hebrew people were not physically asleep. They had been given more than enough provisions to make their journey. They had Moses, called and willing to lead them on the journey. God had even gone so far as to offer them additional incentives of a "thousandfold increase in blessings"! All they had to do was pick up one foot, put it in front of another and make a forward advance. They did not! Why didn't they move out?

The people of God were terrified! The people of God were afraid! The people of God were paralyzed by their collective fear! They were caught in a rut. They were held fast, in place, by what they saw. They got trapped by what they thought. They got snared by their feelings. It's not a new story. Many of us keep missing our "planes" for take-off into tomorrow! Many of us are "asleep" in the airport, at the gate, while the planes keep departing without us. These folks had experience of God being a way maker. They had walked across a huge body of water on dry land. They had been witness to the fact that the enemy who was right behind them had been drowned in a watery grave while trying to catch them and bring them back into slavery. Yet, on the other side of slavery, the people enslaved themselves again! They refused to cooperate with God's strategies for effective change.

Why didn't they move forward? Moses says it plainly in verse 32 of the text: "You did not trust in the Lord your God, who went ahead of you on your journey, in fire by night and in a cloud by day, to search out places for you to camp and to show you the way you should go." Can you believe that we, like the children of Israel, can remain stuck for over forty years and eleven months because of what we see, what we feel, what we think?

An eleven-day journey can stretch into a lifetime of going around in circles because we don't wake up and realize that what we have to offer to our present situation will not move us forward in God. In order to move, in order to grow, in order to stretch, meet the challenge, and advance to the place of divine destiny for your life, it is imperative to heed God's voice and move at the right time.

What will happen if you don't wake up and move out? "Because you wouldn't move, God became angry and declared, 'You shall not enter'." In other words, you will die in a place called "Stuck"! Moses is heartsick about the situation. He is pastor of these people. He has carried them in his heart. He wants to see them make it to the place of promise. So he repeatedly calls out a warning. He continually tries to persuade them to move. He perpetually argues God's case before them. "So I told you, but you would not listen . . ."

We can be told. We can be reminded. We can become better educated. We can become well informed. We can be provided with additional knowledge. We can be given more than enough information. We can hear it. We can read it. We can see it in seven different places via seven alternative methods. And we can remain on an eleven-day journey for over half of our lives, going around and around in circles—because strategy one for advancing is to *act* on what God has said.

God's directives are not up for debate. God's orders are not open to discussion. God's commands are not given for our deliberate consideration. It's real true that God's will for our lives is not always logical, rational, or linear in its seeming design. But if you want to leave the airport terminal and journey on, you have to *act* on the word of God!

The Word of God has to move from being mere words on a page to becoming life that stimulates, motivates, and activates you to move away from the pattern of circles which is taking you nowhere fast! There are many facets of a complex world that tell us that we are alright where we are. We are educated to move only so far. We are culturally socialized to move only so far. The community norms of our immediate area inform our limited movement. Even the Church has planned strategy for our mobility. "This far. No further. It is sin!" But in spite of the many institutional and systemic reasons for our going around in circles, God calls us to move ahead!

God's second strategy is to allow the Living Word to explode within you! You can read the same passage many different times.

You can hear sermons from diverse preachers. You can receive exhortations, teaching, and explanations from a variety of teachers. But one day the words on the page will burst open in your spirit. One day, when you need it the most, there will be this dynamic bursting forth of new life within you. That's the day when the dead letters fragmentize into the living, life-giving Word of spiritual vitality within your very being. What you have heard so many times before finally becomes the Bread of Heaven to you.

I've had this experience. It has felt as though God slipped some new, fresh words onto the pages of Holy Scripture while I was asleep in the night! For although I've seen these very words and have heard them preached on in diverse contexts, the day came when they finally meant something to me!

If you don't "get" this experience, if you remain stuck in place, Deuteronomy 1:45–46 declares that even God will give up on you! "You came back and wept before the Lord, who paid no attention to your weeping and turned a deaf ear to you. And so you stayed in Kadesh many days, all the time you spent there." It hurts to be stuck and to know it. It's painful to watch others moving ahead, accomplishing, achieving, and living the abundant life while you realize that you keep going around in circles. However, weeping and wailing, mumbling and grumbling, whining and complaining will get you nothing and nowhere. Not even God pays attention to our wailing and lamenting if we are not acting, internalizing, and willing to live the Word we have received.

Do you get the message, Sista? I have been deliberate in taking time to walk through a Bible study format to allow this central idea to crystallize within your spirit. What should have and could have been an eleven-day journey was stalled until forty years and eleven months later! Forty years is almost half a lifetime. Forty years is about the time when menopause approaches. Forty years is the point where midlife crises begin to show up and show out. Forty years has given us a variety of life experiences and, hopefully, the ability to explore an assortment of options. So around age forty the Holy Spirit calls out the order to move, to change, to grow, and to fly!

I know from my own personal background that we—women, sisters, daughters of the Most High God—are best known for repeating

STRATEGIES FOR EFFECTIVE CHANGE ❖ 30

our old, familiar patterns in life. We go around in circles, pushing the rewind button to replay, trying to get somewhere while walking on a treadmill. You may feel like you're moving, but actually you're going nowhere fast! Look at the people of color in chapter 2, verse 1 of that same story: "Then we turned back. . . . for a long time we made our way around . . ." The dumb ones were doing the same thing, seeking different results!

We laugh as we say, "Been there, done that." But, while we've been there, we didn't learn the lessons of "there"! While we've done that, the clues we should have got figured out obviously didn't stick! "We turned back . . . and stayed there for a long time." So, God sends the message in the form of a book. God sends a fresh tip to penetrate your spirit. God loves you so much, just the way you are. And God loves you too much to leave you where you are, in the land of Stuck!

Get a clue, Ms. Thang. You have been here long enough! You have cried, yelled, screamed, jumped, shouted, fasted, prayed, and been slain in the Spirit long enough! You have had yourself anointed with enough oil; been to three "Woman Thou Art Loosed" conferences; watched "No More Sheets" with three different sets of girlfriends; slipped off to "get a word" from three different "prophets"; had three zodiac charts done by three folks in worse shape than yourself; bought and read seven different self-help books, including *Lessons in the Valley, In the Meantime, Value in the Valley, Until Today, Woman Thou Art Loosed, The Lady, Her Lover and Her Lord, Inner Healing for Broken Vessels, Taking Back My Yesterdays, Jesus and Those Bodacious Women* along with *Mother Goose Meets a Woman Called Wisdom!* But—and it's a big but—you ain't moved! You have not changed! And you are not doing things differently! Girlfriend, you are still stuck!

God says it loud and clear: You have to move! A song rings in my mind from my childhood that says, "You've got to move." I don't know who sang it. I don't know who wrote it. And at this late date I can't recall what record it was on or where I first heard it. But I can yet hear the words, loud and clear, reminding us that the time in life will come that calls out to us, "You've got to move!"

If you don't move, you will die without ever experiencing abundant life! If you don't move, even God will tire of your tears and pay no further attention to your pleas for help. It is essential that you re-alize that you must cooperate with God's strategies for effective change in your life. Where you are is not your final destination. It's only a layover! Don't go to sleep in the airport and allow the plane to depart without you. A layover is a break time for both you and the plane crew.

There are cheaper airlines that will save us money but not feed us. So during a layover we can stretch our legs from those cramped spaces, go to a full-sized toilet and eliminate waste materials, and find something to sustain us until we arrive at our final destination. On the other hand, the plane has a crew refueling, restocking the juice, pop, and peanuts, as well as cleaning up to allow others on board who are traveling to our final destination.

Everybody is not going to our destination. On layovers people come and go. Some folks deplane never to return. On layovers you can get some things done that will allow you to arrive at your desti-nation without a lot of undue stress. But if you go to sleep during the layover, I'm a witness that the plane will leave your happy behind!

The children of Israel got stuck in the airport, asleep! The ma-jority of them were prevented by God from going to the prepared destination. They got stuck for forty years and eleven months in a layover! The majority of folks who had been delivered from slavery in Egypt stayed enslaved in freedom! It's a sad story. It's a true story. It's a story that is continuing today! Don't let it be your story! It's time for you to make some drastic changes. It's time for you to make some seemingly irrational decisions. It's time for you to be ex-tremely vulnerable and to take some extreme measures in your life. Sista, I'm persuaded that God is ready. The plane of Bodacious Womanist Wisdom is fueled and ready to take off. Are you prepared now to *move?*

WOMAN WISDOM SPEAKS: "Cease listening to Wisdom, and you will stray away from the words of knowledge" (Prov. 19:22).

WOMANIST WISDOM SAYS: If someone else has already done it, you too can repeat it! Womanist Wisdom says that if you thought of it after much fasting, prayer, and meditation, then it's time for you to step off and get going. So what if you have no followers? So what if there is no plan except for the first step? So what if you don't really know where you're headed or what God is doing? So what? God led Abram and Sara out of their home on a wilderness journey and they didn't know either. Did God do alright by them or not?

A BODACIOUS WOMAN will take a giant step of faith! Don't wait to get pushed, my sister . . . move!

4

LITTLE SISTERS AND LITTLE BROTHERS

Song of Solomon 8:8

*Y*ou know and I know that like every race, every culture, every tribe and ethnic group, we have all kinds and sorts and species within the black family. We do most everything and God knows we'll do most anything! We are some of the brightest as well as some of the dumbest.

We are among the most industrious and some of the most trifling. We accomplish some of the most ingenious and creative feats and then turn right around to do something which is awful, hideous, mind-blowing, and incomprehensible. For we are everyone! All families on earth come from us!

When my spouse, Mista Chuck, has a problem with something one of us has done, he will quickly tell me about "your people." It's become a standing joke among us when he tries to back away, stand apart from, and divorce himself from my people. But, I have come to understand that in every family you have and love the good, the bad, the cute, and the ugly!

My aunt used to look at us and ask, "I wonder what you'd look like to me if you were not my family?" Love colors. Love covers. Love includes. Love sees you—dirty, messed up, acting ugly and dumb—and holds onto you and claims you anyhow.

It is a scientific, historical, and religious fact that dysfunction is in every family. There are no exceptions! There are no exclusions. There are no special, privileged families who stand outside of the norm. In some of the most wealthy and well-respected families, known across the world, as well in some of the most poverty stricken families known only to their embarrassed neighbors and the case workers, we find scandal, horror stories, and dysfunctional behaviors.

The Essence Music Festival touts itself as a family event. There is a cross-section of activities and musical artists to satisfy the whole family's tastes. One year I was blessed to be part of this grand event. Chuck and I had front and center VIP seats to hear and see the likes of the grand Pattie LaBelle and Lauren Hill. Essence is known for bringing in headliners who are the creative musical giants, who have a reputation for kickin' it with every note. That year they all brought their best songs—strutted their best stuff—did us proud. Then, one of the family decided to cut the fool!

R. Kelly decided to go straight raunchy. All of the deviant, sexual behavior he exhibited before recording "I Believe I Can Fly" cropped up, multiplied. For demons always multiply when not held in check by the power of the Holy Spirit. Essence pulled the plug on R. Kelly after he had darn near masturbated in public view. He went so far as to pull a black silk sheeted air mattress onto the stage. Susan Taylor, the editorial director of Essence Inc., had them turn off the stage lights and sounds!

Essence Communications went to all the media the next day apologizing for his actions. They said they had invited him because he had claimed to have experienced a spiritual awakening. R. Kelly went from being a favored son to being unveiled as a slave to the troubling spirits that manifest themselves in sexually deviant ways. He is a brilliant lil' brother who is yet part of the family. We own him. We support him by buying his records, tapes, CDs, and videos. We encourage him by buying tickets, attending his concerts, and singing his songs.

If he behaved like this with youth and older adults present, I wonder what he does—how far he goes—at his prime-time events. Folks, this is a family affair. A conference has been called. What does the Word of God have to say about this disturbing family dynamic? I believe we will find an answer in Song of Solomon, chapter 8. This is one of the great love stories of the ancient world recorded for our education, edification, and religious inspiration. We enter the scene after a family conference has been called.

A family conference has been called due to the fact that our little sister has failed to develop breasts. This is a family problem. There is a call for a gathering of all those who are both concerned and involved. For we must put our heads together and take a good look at the identified problem. This situation and all of its explicit implications for a family dilemma is a pressing matter. For if our little sister has no breasts she cannot provide nurture. So what are we going to do? The bridegroom is on the way.

It's a family matter, for it could be an *economic hardship*. The bride's price could be reduced. As a matter of fact, for a woman with no breasts, perhaps there will be a denial or forfeiture of the entire bride's fee. It could cost the family *cultural embarrassment*. Everyone will know that something is wrong with our little sister. It could cost the family *psychological stress*. For apples don't fall far from the tree. And when people discover that we have a breastless sister, they will begin to wonder what is missing or undeveloped about me.

My sister's lack of breasts could cost the family *spiritual anxiety*. For a loving God gives every woman breasts. A loving God wants every woman to be able to nurture both her husband and her children. A loving God would surely want a woman to be able to provide nourishment for her babies. There is an unspoken, unarticulated, and unstated, but very much alive theology that if something is damaged, ill, sick, or deformed, it is a penalty for some sin. The question is raised, why is God angry with our family? Why has God set this affliction in the midst of us? What under-the-table, unknown sin are we being punished for?

And, since we basically serve a "get'm" God, my real spiritual concern when my little sister has no breasts is to be wary and on the alert for when, where, and how God is going to get me. The bottom line is not a genuine regard for my little sister. The bottom line is how can I save my own behind? Come on, family, let's be authentically open, candid, and direct. For I want to know, I need to know, and I m scurrying hard to discover how my sister's lack of breasts impacts me, my safety, my sanity, and, yes, even my salvation. Our collective concern for me causes us to ask the biblical question, what are we going to do?

This Song of Solomon passage sits at the end of a real serious love letter between a man and a woman. They talk of serious, sexual love. We don't know if this is a human exchange or talk about the love of Christ for his bride, the Church of God. It could be either or it could be both. What we do know is that the name of God is not mentioned, but we have a brother who wants to lay his head between the mountains of lilies and a sister who tells him she can hardly wait! At the end of this great discourse on sexual love, we discover that there is a problem. Our little sister has no breasts and the bridegroom will be coming soon.

Let's understand that the concern for our breastless sister is legitimate. For without nourishment an infant cannot survive. All family members, male and female, need sustenance, food, and comfort in order to thrive and develop into their fullest potential. It makes no difference whether a woman has a male or female child, the child needs to be fed. And, since our little sister has no breasts, we have called a family conference.

However, we live in a world that seeks to be politically correct and socially expedient. We no longer use exclusive terms. We have made every attempt to be inclusive. We try to widen the circle. We want to expand our vision. We hope to enlarge our view of the world. So being primarily focused on just our little sister is too limiting. Our being targeted on the breastlessness of a woman is exclusive and not really worthy of all of our conversation. We need to take an inclusive view of the family.

So let's talk about a very dangerous topic. Let's center our attention on a greater concern. It's time to deal with the very real family concern that too many of our little brothers have no balls! So, family, what shall we do?

Foxy Brown, Lil' Kim, and Mary J. Blige are evidence of women who have what the brothers want and think they need. Hooters, boobs, entertainment stations, and luscious spots to rest weary heads—this is what the brothers want.

Now, on the other hand P. Diddy, Heavy D, Busta Rhymes, Silk, and R. Kelly can all wiggle, shake, and intimate that they have the life-giving equipment down in their pants. We cannot see it. We cannot explore the function and adequacy of the equipment they want to make us believe they have. So we could deduce from their posturing that life will flow and new birth will result from any action and activity they initiate.

The biological term for balls is "testes," the seed-producing sacs that store the life force for our race. However, in 'da hood we don't talk about testes. Now, let's be clear that the word, testes, comes from a Latin root word meaning testimony. To testify is to give witness. To testify is to be a sign. To testify is to be a visible symbol of what has happened to us, in us, through us, with us, and oft times in spite of us. The primary function of our brothers' testes is to provide us with the seeds of life. So, family, what happens when our little brother has no balls?

It's a family affair. Without life-giving balls we will cease to exist. A lot of shaking, squirming, and gesturing does not give life. It gives us a false sense of excitement. It makes us feel like passion, romance, and a future is ahead. The moves of implied sexuality and apparent intimacy lead us to a deceiving sense of security. For I want you to be fully aware that our little sister can have a baby without breasts. But a man cannot produce the seed for new life without balls. The biblical question returns. Our little sisters have no breasts—little nurture is going on. Our little brothers have no balls. Life, abundant life, is not happening in the black family. So I call for the question. Family, what are we going to do?

For we can tell that little sisters have no breasts when we see so many yet stuck on stupid, having babies, picking up a welfare check, and dropping the children off at their mothers,' grandmothers,' and sisters.' We can tell they have no breasts when they would prefer to stay in abusive relationships in order to say, "'Dat's my man." We can tell our little brothers are ball-less by their continued violence against women through date rape, abusive language, name calling, nonpayment of child support, and the increase of drug dealers and gang members.

We have a messed-up, complex, and complicated situation to wrestle with today. Family, there is a sense of urgency in this new millennium. As family, we had best wake up and smell the stench! For the survival of our race in health and wholeness is hitting us in the face. There are some immediate steps we need to make.

Families survive and remain intact due to healthy, loving relationships. Families endure the vicissitudes of life because they covenant to stay together in good times and in bad. Families outlive the societal pressures because they continue to hold onto each other and onto God's unchanging hand. God instituted the family. God ordained the family. God designed the family for the perpetuation of our nation, our race, our tribe, and the world. God loved the family so well, so deeply, and so much, that God showed up as Jesus, in a poor, unemployed, migrant family of color. God gave the Life Force, the Testimony, and the Witness to a sin-sick world in the person of Jesus Christ. Jesus was so well-nurtured and nourished by his birth mother that he stopped dying to make room for her in another extended family. God is yet awaiting our response . . . Family, what shall we do?

It is our challenge. It is our quest. It is our mandate to help our sisters develop breasts. It is our job to ensure that our brothers have life-giving balls that testify to God's faithfulness throughout the generations. The work of being concerned about our little sisters and little brothers lies before each of us. The time for swinging, big, augmented, plastic breasts that stimulate, titillate, and excite without feeding the family is over! The time for bumping and grinding, talking loud, and saying nothing has to come to a quick and permanent end. It's time to go back to old, familiar, tested, and tried landmarks that have brought us this far and preserved our family. Sly and the Family Stone as well as the Pointer Sisters say it for me. We are family! With little sisters who have no breasts and little brothers who have no balls, we are still family. It is a family affair. This issue is before us today, for it affects us directly and indirectly.

The church cannot survive without nurture, pastoral care, concern, and our intense personal involvement. We must discover the reason why our little sisters have no breasts. The Church of the Living God will live, regardless of ball-less wonders who try to pass themselves off as real men. God loves us so much, just as we are, breastless and ball-less. And, thankfully, God loves us too much to leave us in this family state of bewilderment and confusion.

Therefore, it is incumbent upon each of us to do our part to save the family. Let's talk about this real-life issue. Let's discover ways to let little sisters and little brothers know that their situation is our immediate concern. And let's fess up that many of us are breastless and ball-less too! We will not allow anyone to be alienated, set aside, talked about, or die all alone, out there, over there, all by herself or himself. We have an obligation to create seminars, workshops, spiritual forums, and safe places where we can discover avenues to allow conversations about this elephant that sits squarely in the middle of our living room.

The elephant is huge. The elephant dung is all across our shared living space. It is foul smelling, unsanitary, and not going away without our collective work to clean up this mess! The time for dysfunction and denial is over. The truth is here. And the truth will make us free to live the abundant life and be nourished as we do it.

My job is to raise a prophetic voice. My task is to call out a clear trumpet sound. My ministry is to uplift our plight and call on God to come quickly to our assistance. Our little sisters have no breasts. Our little brothers have no balls. The day of the bridegroom is approaching. So, family of God, what are we going to do?

WOMAN WISDOM SPEAKS: "Do not be wise in your own eyes. Reverence God and depart from evil. It will be health to your flesh and strength to your bones" (Prov. 3:7–8).

WOMANIST WISDOM SAYS: When you see a sister who needs nurture, don't turn away in disgust; turn to her with compassion! We all need a "breast" to suck every now and then! It's no shame to have a need and a desire for nurture. Most of us didn't get sufficient amounts of nurture from our mothers, for they were too busy working, trying to help keep our homes together. Most of them were not sufficiently nurtured either! For the way of the world has been for women to give, give, give, and give! Now it's time to learn about self-care. Now is the time to teach other women about self-care. Now is the time to ensure that our next generation of little sisters will have breasts! But they can't be what they cannot see in us! Show them how to care for themselves, Wise Woman!

A BODACIOUS WISE WOMAN will invite a needy sister to run away with her for a day of pampering, self-love, and rejuvenation. She will pay for her if she can. This becomes a tithe unto God also!

5

IT'S TIME FOR
A CHANGE!

Jeremiah 29:1–7

The situation is bad. It's getting worse. The child is out of control. The behavior is increasingly bizarre. The doctor can't name the cause. But the pain continues. The marriage is aging. But intimacy is absent. The meetings are predictable. But community is not present. You're studying harder. But the grades don't reflect it. You're talking less. But the arguments are increasing. Communion is served and taken. But love, charity, and harmony are not experienced. The job is there. But no security is felt. Everywhere your life is unpredictable.

All control is gone. You've played your best hand, you're powerless, and you know it. There's no method or strategy working, regardless of how much effort you've employed. You're helpless. You profess it. Finally, you admit that your life is totally unmanageable. You want to run away. But you can't. You want to quit. But you don't dare. You want to give up. But deep down within you there's a teeny-weeny, itsy-bitsy strain of hope.

From somewhere in the recesses of your mind an old tune begins a journey to your spirit. From the ancient storage of your memory the ballad starts to crawl and creep into your consciousness. From the stored tapes of yesterday you begin to literally hear these familiar words of faith playing in your head: *I know a change is gonna come!*

For in the midst of a world of trouble, in a time of perplexing distress, in your worst period of trial, tribulation, and trouble the Holy Spirit will remind you to hold on, hang in there, and not give up—for help is on the way. The words of Scripture come to comfort someone who is going through and has been for a long time. The words of faith come to offer hope and healing for someone who feels discouraged and thinks that God does not care. There is good news for the women of God who are hanging on solely by the hairs on their chinny-chin-chins. God knows how you feel and guarantees you that it's time for a change, and *a change is gonna come.*

Yes, it's time for a change! Thank God for the present and powerful Holy Spirit who comes as our paraclete, our companion, our reminder of the precious promises of Jesus Christ. It may come as a surprise to many, but the truth is that the Holy Spirit doesn't come to just make us jump, run, scream, cry, and shout. The purpose of the Holy Spirit is to remind us of what Jesus said.

After the resurrection, just before he was lifted in ascension to the heavens, Jesus promised his followers, "In a little while you won't see me, but I'm going to send you a comforter. I've got to leave you, but in a little while, I'm going to send you a consoler. I can't remain with you in a physical body, but in a little while, I'm going to send you a helper who will never leave you or forsake you. You won't be able to see me, but in a little while the Holy Spirit will come to live inside of you. I will never leave you or forsake you. And, even when it feels like you're all alone and life seems to have you in a place called down and out . . . hang in there, hold on, don't give up. It may seem like a very long time, but it's time for a change. And you've got to stand still and know—*a change is gonna come!*

This oldie but goody is a song, written and first performed by Sam Cooke during the civil rights era.[1] It's a song written to people of color who have been enslaved in the land of the free and the home of the slave. It's a song written to folks whose parents and grandparents knew what it meant to work from sunup to sundown, with no pay and little food, for folks who watched their family members be sold, their loved ones killed, their community constantly destroyed, and their dreams for a peaceful promised land dashed over and over.

It's a song for those who know about separate and unequal, those who are well acquainted with the back of the bus, the colored washrooms, and colored water fountains. It's a song for those who could cook the food and yet not be served at those restaurants. It's a song for those who could clean the rooms in big, spacious houses but never rent or own one in a decent part of town. It's a song of faith in a God who is faithful to every promise written in the Book of record.

Regardless of how long you've been going through, no matter how painful the situation that has been holding onto the anchors of your heart, despite the fact that it seems as if even Almighty God has forgotten your name, address, birthday, and social security number . . . in spite of the reality that you've fasted, prayed, touched, and agreed with seven prayer partners (Yes, you've been anointed with oil, been slain in the Spirit, and fasted for three lunch hours), the devil wants you to believe that where you are is the end of the line. The enemy of our soul wants to trap you into feeling that this is the awful place designed to take you down. But you've got to know and you've got to know that you know: *a change is gonna come, oh yes it will.*

The passage from the prophet Jeremiah is a story about faith in action. It's a story of hope in the very face of a long and horrible enslavement and confinement. The people of God were exiled to a foreign land. The Church of God was sitting in a guarded retention camp, while Jerusalem had been captured and occupied by the Babylonians. In a time of trouble and tribulation, a word came from God. Jesus declared that "my sheep know my voice." In the midst of problematic circumstances, God will speak to you. In the very time of seemingly hopeless and alarming predicaments, God will speak. In the very eye of the whirling storm, with junk, debris, and all types of garbage being tossed to and fro in your life, God will speak.

For God is not silenced by our troubles. God does not hush because Satan is cutting the fool. God is not voiceless because there seems to be no way out. Friends, when you are going through, be on the alert, for God will speak.

"A Change Is Gonna Come" was written as a song of faith. It is a song of hope. It is a song about rocking steady and being determined not to give up. It is a song to encourage those who knew long, sleepless, tearful nights and days filled with gloom and cloudy skies. This song is a word of hope to stormy weather people, sitting in the midst of a torrential downpour of hatred, captivity, and severe mistreatment. It's a song written to say, don't just watch the rain. But, while it's pouring, thundering, and flashing lightning, that is the time to stretch your neck and begin to look for the rainbow. This song says, don't allow situations to cause you to hang your head in hopelessness. But while the devil is acting up, you begin to look up in faith.

Yes, it's been a long time since the Middle Passage and the auction blocks. Yes, it's been a long time since African Americans have lived on plantations and were known as "happy darkies." And, yes, it's been a long time since Reconstruction and empty promises. Notwithstanding, it's been a long time since civil rights were pledged and then reneged upon, time after time after time. With all of this being our truth, our task is to hold on to the Living Word of God! In the midst of dire straits, difficult days, dwindling finances, messed-up relationships, and uncooperative folks, both at home and on the job, if we hold on to the truth of the God who never fails, if we keep faith in the God of yesterday, today, and tomorrow, it may have been a long time, but know this day that change has got to come!

Jeremiah heard God clearly. Jeremiah understood that he was going to sound foolish. Jeremiah was sure that what God was commanding wouldn't make sense to all of the Church members sitting in captivity, away from their promised land. But when God spoke, Jeremiah wrote. When God spoke, Jeremiah purposed to call out this crazy plan laid down by God. When God spoke, Jeremiah provided the strategy for change to come their way.

"Thus says the Lord of hosts, the God of Israel, to all the exiles whom I have sent into exile from Jerusalem to Babylon: 1) Build houses and live in them; plant gardens and eat what they produce. 2) Take wives and husbands. Have children in order that they may bear children. 3) Multiply there and do not decrease. 4) Seek the welfare of the city where I have sent you into exile. 5) Pray to the Lord on behalf of the place where you are in captivity. 6) Know that in its welfare you will find your welfare" (Jer. 29:1–7).

You've got to see the picture. Israel was a backsliding nation. Babylon had kicked their behinds once again. Their promised land had been taken away by foreign invaders. Jewish leadership had been rounded up, deported, and locked up in Babylon. Their homes had been confiscated. Their property had been divided among the conquerors. Their temple had been desecrated. Jerusalem now lay in ruins. It looked like the Church was down and out.

For forty long years, under five kings, Jeremiah had preached "repent or be doomed." For forty long years this messenger of God had preached, but the people had refused to listen. For forty long years Jeremiah had stood alone, weeping and wailing over the conditions of a backsliding heifer named Israel. Understand that Jeremiah was not a T. D. Jakes. No one wanted to hear him preach. Jeremiah was not a Paul Morton. People didn't flock to his Full Gospel, "six-in-one" conventions. Jeremiah was not a Creflow Dollar. He was considered a miserable failure by popular standards. Jeremiah never attained material success. He underwent severe deprivation. The old boys club turned on him, plucked out his beard, and threw him in a pit. His neighbors rejected him and the ministerial alliance wouldn't allow him membership. But Jeremiah was faithful to God. Jeremiah was committed to God. Jeremiah was courageous. Jeremiah was bodacious. And Jeremiah knew the voice of God. So he wrote to the people in exile with a plan from God.

Essentially, God told the Church to invest in a foreign land. "You are in exile. Don't expect quick deliverance and microwave escape! This is a situation that you got yourself into by your own choices. Your current position is one that you earned due to your willful disobedience to the will of God. Now that you're in hot water, don't expect me to hurry up, come quick, get there right now, and fix the mess you're in. But I do have a plan for you while you're in the mess you made, to contribute to your own deliverance. While it feels like your heart is going to break, cooperate with the plan of action I've laid out. Take some risks even when you don't understand my thinking. For my ways are not your ways. My thoughts are not your thoughts." But God does have the better and best idea.

We don't have to understand the logic. We don't need to be able to figure it out. The plan is to stop whining, stop complaining, stop grumbling and mumbling, and do something different. Put something of yourself into the mess you've made. Invest in building up your own house. Stop tearing down what's not going right. Stop pulling apart what you don't like. Give something. Offer something. Invest where you are. Plant where you are. Cultivate where you are. God never promised to come and fix Israel's situation. God told them to work in the place they found themselves.

Marriage not working? Invest. Take a class on communications and conflict resolution. Children acting crazy? Invest. Take an effective parenting class. Learn to listen. Illness getting you down? Invest in speaking well to yourself; stop claiming sickness; begin to stretch your body; exercise your temple; pamper yourself. Church ain't what you like? Speak out and offer suggestions; find a need and offer to fill it; come to a board meeting and lend a hand. School going crazy? Teachers ignoring you? Invest in a computer class; learn more; impress them; show them how much you will learn in spite of them. Singleness getting to you? Invest in you. Network. Mentor children who will love to see you and accept whatever you have to offer. The situation will not get any better until you really decide to go to work and invest yourself.

God says multiply. Your child acting a fool? Plant what you have to offer into the lives of other children who appreciate and love you. Stop trying to buy your children's love. Invest what you have wherever it will be received. All children belong to us. We are all connected. You are not simply responsible for the children you brought into the world. Can't have a child? Invest in one of the too many who have no parent. Take a class. Start a group. Join a study club and improve your mind. Join an exercise program and invest in your health. Organize a group. Teach something that you specialize in and be blessed. You have to multiply. God has decreed that we have to increase and not decrease. If the folks around you won't accept your gifts, there are some folks who are crying out, praying, and asking God to send you their way. There are many captives who need what you have to invest.

People of God, we are in the right place, wherever we are! For the steps of the righteous are ordered by God. People of God, there is no spot where God is not! God is even in the tough situation you're currently in. People of God, the strategy for getting out of a bad situation is laid out before us. It is God's plan. And we have to work this plan.

Yes, it's been a long time coming, but "a change is gonna come" when we work God's plan. Wherever you are, God says seek the welfare of the place that you are in. Pray for the ones causing you pain. Pray for the ones causing you hurt. Pray for the very place you want to leave!

Seek the welfare of the very place where you have been exiled, says God. And it's not to be a prayer of curse and damnation. It's to be a prayer for blessing. The prayer is simple: "God bless this situation. God bless this person. God bless this mess." God doesn't need your specifics. God doesn't need our directions. We have simply been commanded to pray for the welfare, benefit, and best good of the people, place, or situation around us. It doesn't make sense. It doesn't seem fair. It doesn't feel just. But it's God plan.

For when we pray for the welfare of those who hold us in exile, God has promised that we will find our best good! When we pray for those who despitefully use us, God promises to intervene on our behalf. Folks, it's time to get busy. It is praying time!

Sista Linda, that sounds nice and biblical. But you don't know my situation. You couldn't possibly have a clue about the mess I'm going through. There is no way you can tell me that my problem is going to get better. I've done everything humanly possible. I've strategized, networked, organized, plotted, planned, cussed, fussed, fallen out, and decided to throw up my hands in disgust. There is no way something so simple can get me out of the place I'm in.

Sista Friend, this passage of scripture comes at just this point in our lives. For our extremity is God's opportunity to show up and to show out. When we decide that God actually does know more than we do, we can follow the plan and sit back and wait for God to work. It's been a long time coming, but a change has got to come, when you follow God's plan for deliverance.

For more than three years I worked in the annual conference offices of our denomination in West Michigan. For more than three years I had to endure two different white supervisors trying to persuade the bishop to dismiss me. For three years I had people come into my office and give me suggestions about different positions in different parts of the world where there were "good jobs for me"! For more than three years the enemy sought ways to entrap me, bring me down, and put out the fire and passion in my spirit. For more than three years it was extremely painful. For more than three years it was terribly disappointing. But God said to me, "Girlfriend, work the plan." God said to me, "Sista, work the plan." God said to me, "While it hurts like hell, build houses and invest in the midst of your captivity. Multiply and don't decrease. Don't you let the devil take your joy and make you stifle the gifts I've given you." So my husband and I purchased a mortgage! In the midst of hell we invested in West Michigan.

Seek the welfare of West Michigan. Plant trees right there. Plant shrubs right there. Plant flowers right there. Put your children in homes and schools in West Michigan. Seek the welfare of West Michigan. And pray for the folks who are acting like heathens in West Michigan. Pray for the very ones who want you to disappear. Pray their blessing. Pray their highest good. Pray their best benefit. For as you pray for them, God promised, "I'll lift you up." As you pray for their wellness and bless them, God promised, "I'll bless you, prosper you, and take you before those in authority so you can expose the evil one." As I prayed for the welfare of West Michigan, my personal welfare was tied to it.

I couldn't run. I couldn't look for another position somewhere else. I couldn't even take my supervisors to court and sue them for racial discrimination, although I had an excellent case. Our Savior, who went to Calvary as a captured criminal, looked down at those who were doing him harm and prayed for their welfare! "God forgive them their ignorance of who I am," Jesus prayed, and so did I.

Oh, I've not always been so good. I've done my own share of dirt. But somebody prayed for me. They had me on their mind and took the time to pray for me. I'm so glad they prayed. I pray that they continue to pray. For although it was a long time in coming, I'm persuaded, I'm convinced, I'm convicted, and deep down in my heart I do believe that my change has come! God had to move me out in order to move me up! God's plan worked for me!

Sista, when you work God's plan, it will work for you! I guarantee you this is mighty, mighty good news!

WOMAN WISDOM SPEAKS: "Keep sound wisdom and discretion; so they will be life to your soul and grace to your neck. Then you will walk safely in your way, and your foot will not stumble. When you lie down, you will not be afraid; yes, you will lie down and your sleep will be sweet. Do not be afraid of sudden terror, nor of trouble from the wicked when it comes; for the Lord will be your confidence and will keep your foot from being caught" (Prov. 3:21–26).

WOMANIST WISDOM SAYS: Go back and read the story again! Read it slowly this time.

A BODACIOUS WOMAN would work God's plan! It's filled with wisdom, good advice, and sound doctrine for your movement ahead! You go, girl!

6

FREED TO STAND

Luke 13

*T*he deed was done! The words were out! There was no taking them back! I had broken the silence, told the family secret, and announced the incest to the world. For the sake
of my own inner healing, for the restoration of my broken
self, and for my need to be cleansed and made whole, I had decided
to remain a victim no longer. I declared my own liberation. I forged
my own reconstruction. I announced my own benediction upon the
abuse that had held me bound for so long. But it wasn't the end.

I had struggled for so long to be whole. The journey from victim
to survivor was not easy. Many wonderful folks had walked, cried,
laughed, and carried me along the way. Counseling, therapy,
Clinical Pastoral Education, small groups, and healing circles had
all helped in the process that led me to break the silence of incest. I
felt good about my progress. A load of guilt and shame had been
lifted. I could see the sun beginning to shine upon my life. There
was hope ahead. And I was running to embrace it, with joy. Not only
had I told the story of a shameful past, but I had written an article
for *Sage, A Scholarly Journal For Black Women*. This article had been
solicited by Evelyn White for inclusion in her work *The Black*

Woman's Health Book. The "world" knew my secret and it was alright with me.

When Evelyn sent me two copies of the book, I invited my three sisters to come to my home for a celebration. I was excited about the work that black women had accomplished in telling our own stories. I was ready to shout, to dance, and to rejoice. But, my sisters were not happy! When they walked into the house I gave them copies of the book, turned to my name in print. I thought they would honor this giant step in my life and growth. I was prepared for laughter and the whooping that was to come from my family. The outcome surprised me. My sister next to me was outraged and did not hesitate to tell me so. She grabbed the book to her breast as the tears began to roll, and she demanded that I follow her into the toilet.

"How dare you write about my life! Who gave you permission to tell this story when I have not even told the man I'm going to marry?" I stuttered and stammered, trying to find the words to explain that this was my story that I told and that she was only a participant. I was hurt. I was shocked. I was angry. I stomped back down the stairs to get the reaction of my other sisters. They, too, were reluctant to deal with the truth of our dysfunctional family. They knew the truth, yet they wanted me to continue the lie. Even though both of our parents were dead, there was this hesitation to "pull the covers back" and look at our lives.

There are eight siblings in my family, four sisters and four brothers. So knowing my sisters unfavorable reactions made me realize that my brothers would be a greater force to reckon with because they had idolized my father. One brother lived in Switzerland and another in Alaska, but they had to be faced. I needed to know their feelings. I needed their support and love. For I'm the oldest, the inherited matriarch, and I refused to watch our close family ties disintegrate. There was no apology on my part. The deed was done. The words were out. There was no taking them back. But reconciliation had to be achieved. Another process for healing lay ahead.

The world is filled with people who are broken, fragmented, and hurting. Far too many of us live empty lives, mouth empty meaningless phrases, and know that we have a hole in our own souls aching to be filled. We want something. We search for something. We look for something and even someone who will make us feel wanted, needed, desired, and worthwhile. I knew this search personally. I wanted my siblings to make the journey to healing with me. Each of us had been bent over and bowed by the situation in our home. The self-esteem of my entire family had been attacked by the demon of incest. Each one of them had not been raped, but each one of them had been affected by the atmosphere of secrecy and lies.

The most active demon alive in the world of black people is that one who robs us of our self-esteem, the one who steals our self-worth, the one who kills our confidence in our future. I submit to you that the issue of low self-esteem is the most crucial problem that black women face. And the issue of low self-esteem is always present in the life of an abuse victim. Although we are created in the image of the Divine, valued, esteemed, and cherished by God, the sin of abuse ruptures our lives and affects the way that we see ourselves. Remember the bowed head and timid demeanor of Celie in *The Color Purple*.

Abuse causes an interior threat to your sense of security and causes you to live in quiet terror and enormous fear. The root of that fear comes from your self-worth, your personal value, and your human dignity being threatened. Shame, insecurity, self-negation, and self-hatred cause us to walk bent over and bowed down. But there is another reality. There is another way to live. I had found the path and was not going to regress. And, I wanted my siblings to find their way. I had lived the life of the bent-over woman in the Scriptures and my written testimony was the praise to God that she gave for being delivered to stand up straight.

That Gospel passage in Luke 13 details a sister who had been crippled by a spirit of affliction for eighteen years. Contrary to most interpretations that we have heard, she was not physically ill. The Bible says that Girlfriend had a spirit who had made itself at home in her. Even though we have become very sophisticated, educated, and cultured, the demonic is alive and well. We need a clear understanding that the enemy of our souls sends evil spirits to our homes, our jobs, our churches, and our social gathering places. An evil spirit will take up residence in each one of us. Shocking, isn't it? But abuse and violence are not from God! They are the personification of evil, which attacks our physical selves and then settles into our minds, our emotions, our hearts, and our spirits.

Many of us have become emotional, spiritual, and psychological cripples. Some of us are miserable and make everybody around us crazy. Some of us have no sense of what it means to be whole, to be healed, or to be saved from the torture of the evil spirit of abuse. For the first forty years of my life, this was my reality. But the time comes when the evil has to turn you loose!

The day arrives when you realize that Jesus has already dealt with the demonic on our behalf! If we are willing to work on our own behalf, if we are willing to cooperate with the healing process, we can be delivered. For it makes no difference to God whether we are afflicted by a spirit of inner poverty, which feels like a broken spirit; awful shame of unbearable grief; guilt, suicidal depression; or a spiritual weakness that keeps kicking your backside. God wants us to be whole. It does not matter that you have an inferiority complex and feel unlovable or if you like yourself or not, healing is possible. We don't have to remain bent over or bowed down.

Struggling, searching, groping for something to hang onto, I came to the realization that Jesus was concerned about me. When my family had failed to be the nurturing arms that I needed, supportive people were sent into my life. For, as he saw the bent-over woman, Jesus saw me and my pain. For there is no spot where God is not! Write this down. Tape it to the mirror over your wash basin. Place it on the door of the refrigerator. And glue it to the dashboard of your car. When the bent-over woman could not see Jesus, he saw her. This assurance allowed me to know that God is watching over us. In spite of the circumstances and despite the situations, Jesus sees and he cares.

After seeing the sister who had been bent and bowed for eighteen years come into the temple, Jesus called her. "Softly and tenderly," the songwriter says, we continue to be called by the One who wants to see us healed. When things are going their worst, if we would learn to stop, be still, and listen, we would hear that soft-spoken voice speaking peace to our broken spirits. But when the noise and the clamor of foolishness begin, we heed their call and forget that there is another voice.

When my sister began to cry and get angry, I matched her emotions and got angry too. Then when I sat to ponder why she was so upset, when I stopped to consider what had prevented her from giving me a "firm high five," the still small voice spoke into my spirit.

Howard Thurmond says that if we can "center down" we will be able to attend to this gentle voice. The Sweet Spirit of Gentleness reminded me that I had moved from my old place, and that I needed to bring along my siblings with love and with compassion. When the voice registered in my spirit, I knew that I was free from the old evil spirit that used to live in me!

Jesus said to our sister, "Woman, you are free from your ailment." This was a command of liberation. It was the breaking of yokes. It was the falling away of the chains that had held her bound for those many years. I can remember the time that my ego strength was so fragile that I could not deal with anger directed against me. I can remember the time that my self-confidence was so low that I could not stand to be confronted with another's truth. I would take it in and "own" it as mine. But my journey had led me to a new place. I was free from the ailment of abuse which had robbed me and held me bent over and bowed down for so many years. My siblings had problems with my liberation. But I was free!

Liberation means that new opportunities await you. Liberation means that unlimited potential is ahead of you. Liberation means that new beginnings are in store for you. After Jesus spoke to our sister, he touched her and she stood up straight! It's so important to have a circle of support where you can be touched. It was essential for me to have a group of sisters who could reach out to me with empowering words, directions, and counsel when my blood sisters failed me.

This is why we reach out and touch each other when we pray. This is why we dare to lay hands on each other. For touching imparts healing, and healing belongs to the people of God. Touching is the means by which we convey to each other the restorative ministry of Jesus Christ. With a touch of power, Girlfriend was no longer the bent-over woman!

My family enters this story at this point and so do many of yours. For when Jesus had healed the woman and allowed to her to stand up straight, many folks in the temple had the audacity to become indignant because she had been delivered! It lets us know that everybody does not want to see us get well! There are family members, church members, coworkers, business associates, and social aquaintances who want us to remain bound and bent over.

For people know how to work our nerves. People know how to push our buttons. People know just what makes us tick. If we get well, what will they do? If we get well, who will be the fool in the midst? If we get well, who will they have to look down on and feel sorry for? If we get well, who will be identified as the "crazy one" in the group? I had played a significant emotional and financial role in my family of origin. I had contributed much out of my need to be loved, appreciated, and looked up to, which soothed my low self-esteem. If I was going to stand up and be straight, who would or could take over my role?

Jesus called the Church leaders hypocrites! Then he questioned them, "Ought not this daughter of Abraham, whom Satan bound for eighteen years, be set free form this bondage . . . ?" The message in this question was that in the plan of God there is healing. In the plan of God there is deliverance. In the plan of God there is room for the sick, the ill, and the afflicted. Each of us has some acceptable reason for being crippled and bent over.

But in the plan of God our excuses do not work. We can no longer point the finger at our past, our parents, or any of our deficits. For it is the plan of God that we move into a healing space. Movement will require helpers. Movement will call for our involvement. Movement will bring misunderstanding. Movement will cause tension and another type of pain. When birth occurs, there must be pain!

It was painful for me to stand up to my siblings and repeat over and over again, "This is my truth! I have a right to tell my story!" It was painful to realize that they could not celebrate my movement. But the plan of God was in effect in my life. I had a new name! I was not the bent-over woman anymore! As Patti Labelle declared, I had "a new attitude!"

The sister did not leave the temple the same way that she entered. Jesus called her "daughter." Jesus acknowledged their relationship as blood kin. He enlarged the circle and made room for her.

He reminded the temple leaders that since this woman was related to Abraham she had every right to all of the benefits of the covenant. For the covenant binds us to God, and all God has belongs to me. The covenant says that when Jesus died on Calvary he died for me. When he rose in victory, it meant that every evil spirit had already been conquered on my behalf.

Dorothy Norwood sings my theme song, which says "Victory is mine. Victory is mine. Victory today is mine. I told Satan to get thee behind, for victory today is mine."[1] I refused to be bent again with the emotional entanglements of my siblings. I would not allow them to pull me back into my former bent-over condition. So, walking in victory, I called the ones stateside together and they heard me declare that with them or without them, I was going to remain on the journey to inner healing.

This journey meant writing the story, sharing the story, and telling the story of freedom, healing, and victory everywhere I went. Then my husband and I traveled to both Alaska and Switzerland to visit with my other brothers. Family secrets cannot be dealt with on the phone! It required hours and hours of talk, tears, and sharing memories. But the happy ending is that they can each celebrate my freedom today! The happy ending is that some of them came to new avenues of truth for themselves. The happy ending is that most of them are on the healing journey for themselves!

In the story of the bent-over woman, I noticed that all of the initiative for healing was on the part of Jesus. Jesus did not want to see her or us bent over or bowed down. Since you have picked up this book, since you are reading this story, know that Jesus has seen your pain. Jesus has called your name. Jesus desires to touch you, to set you free, and to give you a new name and a new journey toward wholeness. Let your healing process continue! For you don't have to remain bent over or bowed down. Victory can be yours!

WOMAN WISDOM SPEAKS: "Let your heart retain my words. Keep my commands and live. Get wisdom! Get understanding! Do not forget or turn away from the words of my mouth. Do not forsake her, and she will preserve you; love her, and she will keep you. Exalt her, and she will promote you; she will bring you honor when you embrace her. She will place on your head an ornament of grace; a crown of glory she will deliver to you" (Prov. 4:4–9).

WOMANIST WISDOM SAYS: Follow your own path. Many times you will walk alone, it will seem. But, you are actually never alone. For Jesus has promised to never leave you nor to forsake you. The poem "Footprints" has been carried to an extreme in many instances. But its reality is worth taking note of when we feel forsaken. For when we take a step and walk into places where "fools dare not tread," it is there that we will be carried. Because we must go through! There is no easy way to our divine destiny. The bumps are what lift us to higher heights.

A **BODACIOUS WOMAN** would have a copy of *Hinds Feet On High Places* by Hannah Hurnard on her night stand to remind her of the many and varied paths we must travel when we work for the Good Shepherd.

7

CAN YOU WITNESS TO PEACE?

Luke 24:36-48

*H*annah Hurnard knew about the life of Christian people. Hannah was a woman who was familiar with our desire to go to heights unknown with God. She also recognized the reality of sinking into the pits of despair. Hannah fully comprehended the many times we attempt to do good—to live right and to make quality decisions. She understood how we fail, falter, and make poor choices for our lives. Hannah had firsthand acquaintance with fear, confusion, and anxiety. She dared to put her story in print as she wrote the book *Hinds Feet On High Places.*

This allegory recounts the life of a little sheep with crippled feet whose name was, appropriately, Much Afraid. She desperately wanted to work for the Chief Shepherd and journey to the high places. The more she talked about her desire, the crazier her family felt she had become. They wanted her to get married and to settle down. So the family chose her a mate, a distant cousin whose name was Craven Fear.

Now Much Afraid realized that this marriage would be certain death for her. So she ran away and the Shepherd found her. Knowing her fragile condition caused by her crippled feet, the Shepherd promised her two companions to journey with her to the heights. Their names were Suffering and Sorrow. They were solemn in dress, somber in attitude, and could not talk. But these three set out on the journey.

Can you imagine Much Afraid traveling with Suffering and Sorrow? How far can this trio travel before chaos, tears, and self-pity join them and wreck the trip? Isn't this the story of our lives? And surprisingly, it's the story of the Church. Those who made up the first Church of Jesus Christ were folks who were much afraid, filled with sorrow over the loss of their Teacher, and hiding in an upper room to evade personal suffering.

It's almost inconceivable that the Church of Jesus Christ began with a group of scared, terrified, and hiding folk, locked in a room. Trained and taught by the Divine Instructor, they didn't have anything to say. These are the folks who had traveled the countryside for three and a half years, but now they were sitting, much afraid, paralyzed with fear.

Can you imagine this motley crew of timid soldiers, reluctant warriors, and speechless messengers, whose greatest act of courage was to get up, board up the windows, and ensure that the bolts on the door were secure? This gathering had to have been one of pure introspection. This had to have been a time of true confession. They may have looked out the windows, but they couldn't look at each other. They were forced to look within themselves. For in the night, in the quiet time, comes that period of raw and honest self-examination.

They had made promises but had broken every one. They were guilty. When the Roman soldiers took Jesus, his followers had quietly taken off. They were guilty. With newly washed feet, the sacramental wine of New Covenant, and the bread of Christ personal sacrifice as recent memories, their declarations of devotion and loyalty had become blatant lies. They were truly guilty. When the roll had been called at the crucifixion, all but one had been absent. When the blood of remission met the water for renewal at the foot of the cross, they had been absent. They were guilty of missing the birthing of the Church simply because they were much afraid, filled with sorrow, and desperately trying to avoid any suffering.

But they couldn't forget their guilt. They couldn't forget their fear. And they couldn't forget Jesus.

So they sat in a room, frightened, guilty, and needing to confess. But there was no Savior to hear their confession. There was no Comforter to soothe their fears. And there was no Redeemer to absolve their guilt. They could have sung songs, but there would have been no praise. They could have told stories, but there would have been no power. They could have called a committee meeting, but there was no community. There was just a group of frightened disciples, much afraid, filled with sorrow, and desperately trying to avoid suffering.

Yet when the guilt overwhelmed them, when the craven fear caused them to tremble, when the sorrow over their failures was eating away at their core, there was suddenly a voice that cried, "Peace be with you!"

Every head lifted. Every eye turned. Every mouth dropped opened. There he stood. The door was still locked. But—surprise, surprise—there he stood. The stone couldn't keep him in the tomb, and locked doors couldn't keep him away from this sad bunch. Our fears and failures, intermingled with our unconfessed sins, won't keep him away from us either. Get ready. Be on the alert. You just might be in for a grand surprise. Jesus had warned them that they would betray him, but they had not agreed. Jesus had warned them that the evil one sought to sift them, separate them, and divide them like wheat, but they had not agreed. Jesus had foretold of his suffering, trial, death, and resurrection, but they had not agreed. Jesus had also known they were much afraid. Jesus had known they were filled with sorrow and remorse. Jesus had understood their reluctance to journey through suffering. And Jesus had known that they would need this time to reach the point of confession. For confession means to agree with God. As they sat, locked in this room, Jesus knew they were now ready to agree with God that good people, lots of ideas, many good intentions, financially secured budgets, decent programs, well-attended seminars, and even Ph.D.'s in theology are not enough to build a faith community. Something had been missing and, as always, Jesus came to meet the needs of these, his fearful friends.

When they were empty, filled with pain; when they were discouraged, filled with doubt; when they were hopeless, feeling it was the end, Jesus came and spoke, "Peace be with you!" Oh, how many times I've been where the disciples were. Oh, how numerous are the times I've failed my Savior. Oh, how often have I forgotten his words of promise and gone against his design for my life.

No, I've never turned my back completely and walked away from Christ. But I did begin trying my own devices, seeking my own revenge, and I neglected turning to God for direction or guidance.

No, I've never cursed God's name, but I have refused to offer praise as I grumbled, whined, and complained.

No, I've never failed to assemble with the people of God, but I have at times only assembled to find fault, to point blame, and to pick apart the assembly. I've come to recognize that I do these things when I get filled with fear; when sorrow is my constant companion, and when I think my personal suffering ought to be over!

But what a friend we have in Jesus! All our sins and unconfessed pains he wants to bear. Comes the midnight hour, filled with thundering quiet and sleepless nights. Comes the midnight hour when the roaring solitude allows my false bravado to disappear and my public mask to be removed. Comes the midnight hour with the full recognition that I've played all my cards, tried all my tricks, used every resource, and my back is still up against the wall. Comes the midnight hour and I acknowledge my wrong, confess my sin, seek forgiveness, and hear a surprising small voice whisper, "Peace be with you, Linda!"

Jesus didn't enter that room with recriminations and accusations. Jesus did not approach them with "I told you so" speeches or even with questions that probe, hurt, and penetrate. Rather, when they saw themselves for what they were, when they could confess their inadequacies and insufficiencies without Jesus, it was then that he came with what they needed most—peace, shalom, all that made for their good.

Much afraid disciples can be renewed and restored. Suffering and sorrow can be put within the context of growth, development, and expanding potential. Speechless tongues can issue praise. Locked doors can open and the message of redemption can be taken to a hurting world, for Jesus will come, speaking peace, bringing joy, stretching smiles, and placing twinkles where tears have flowed. Makes no difference who you are or what you've done, Jesus will come, hanging bright stars in gloomy skies, arching rainbows in the midst of thunderstorms, causing flowers to bloom in even your desert places. When Jesus comes, he will call you by name.

The story of Much Afraid, Suffering, and Sorrow is the story that we live. Their experience is about our journey to the high places in God. The good news is that each one of them got a new name. When they finally reached the high place, the Shepherd named them Love, Joy, and Happiness. In the same manner, those disciples in that upper room experienced the personal victory of confessing failure and receiving amazing grace! For the peace that Jesus brings is the power of the Holy Spirit, which will send us forth with a surprising new testimony of proclamation: "He lives. He lives. Christ Jesus lives today. He walks with me and talks with me along life's narrow way. He lives. He lives, salvation to impart. You ask me how I know he lives?" He's spoken peace to my failures, received my confession, and now "he lives within my heart!"[1]

WOMAN WISDOM SPEAKS: "The reverence of the Lord is the instruction of wisdom, and before honor is humility" (Prov. 15:33).

WOMANIST WISDOM SAYS: We can live hearing the sweet gentle voice of "Peace." We do not have to live in the midst of constant drama! Too many of us are attracted to the mess that we have lived in with our family of origin. We don't have to live this way! When we decide that enough is enough, God will break into our lives with better than we have ever imagined! The issue is having a desire to change!

A BODACIOUS WOMAN would work to be at peace with herself, her surroundings, and her God. She would fill her space with fresh flowers at least weekly, burn aromatherapy candles, and display beautiful artifacts and delightful pictures to help her settle down. Once a month she would go and take a massage, a facial, a pedicure, and manicure. I worked for many months to purchase a two-seat jacuzzi, which is lovely, simply lovely. Mista Chuck put it in for a Christmas gift! It's a jewel. My friend Rev. Brenda J. Little says that we all need to make creative quiet spots and times for ourselves. These things all help the drama to cease and desist. Work on it. It will work for you!

8

IF IT HAD NOT
BEEN FOR ME!

2 Kings 5

*I*f you search long enough, dig deep enough, "read on" and look intensely, you'll find all sorts of women's truths hidden away in Scripture. There is something to uplift and encourage women of all ages. We don't hear their stories often enough. We don't have a lot of information provided about them. But what the "forefathers" allowed into the canon gives serious clues about the importance of their lives.

In every book I write there will be stories for my "lil sistas." I have a daughter, Grian Eunyke, and a granddaughter, Symphony Markelia. It is important that I recall how life has not always been kind to me, that I write hoping their's will be better. It is essential that I remember the wisdom passed on to me by my foremothers and leave it for my girls.

Today, I can only recall some of the lessons of my matriarchs. Time has erased much of their wisdom; events have clouded and twisted what they said with what I've picked up, read, and experienced along the way. So I am forced to leave something in print, for I am already one of the ancestors of tomorrow!

As I have sat in conversation with biblical women, trying to see what ones to include in this work, a young slave girl jumped up, demanding I hear her voice. I was busy writing about adults who were "serious sistas" when Ms. Mouth wouldn't shut up or go away. She has been silent and unnamed too long. She has been invisible like many domestics. But she was insistent that I tell her story and bring her to life.

Second Kings chronicles the downward spiral of Israel in the period of time following King David's death. The nation was divided. God had called out a serious warning to the people! "The Lord warned Israel and Judah through the prophets and seers: 'Turn from your evil ways. Observe my commands and decrees in accordance with the entire Law that I commanded.' But they would not listen and were as stiff-necked as the previous generations who did not trust in the Lord their God" (2 Kings 17:13–14).

It is not known who collected the history recorded in these two legends of successive kings of Israel. Scholars have attributed these stories to Jeremiah or even to those unnamed males who attended "the schools of the prophets." What we do know is that as the people of God wandered off into idolatry and corruption, the former glory of God was withdrawn and they found themselves embroiled in many wars, which they lost. Their people were captured.

One of their most vicious enemies was the army of Aram. The Arameans were a major source of frustration and political upheaval. In their constant raids upon Israel, they took many captives to Aram and forced many into slavery. One little Israelite girl was made a servant to the wife of Naaman, an Aramean army commander.

Like most of the women and girls in Scripture, Lil' Sista is unnamed. We are not given any physical description or genealogical background. The Bible doesn't record how she became a servant. The only thing we're told is that "bands of Aram had gone out and had taken a young girl from Israel and she served Naaman's wife" (2 Kings 5:2).

This is enough to know. Domestic work has been a way of life for women of color since the very beginning. The work is hard. The

days are long. The duties are repetitive. The results are unappreci-
ated. The workers are all but invisible!

I've been reading a series by Barbara Neely, an African American
woman who has made an art of writing about being a "domestic."
Her protagonist, Blanche White, is a hoot. Girlfriend is forty-two, single, adoptive mother of two, sassy, determined, sharp, and intelligent.
Blanche appears first in *Blanche on the Lam*. She returns in *Blanche
and the Talented Tenth*. The final sequel is *Blanche Cleans Up*.

Blanche "knows" her business. She sizes up a house and its own-
ers in short order. She can assess personalities from food preference,
bedroom decor and bathroom habits. She has a keen perception and
can unearth what many would prefer to leave buried. For as a domestic worker, Blanche sees her employees raw. At home, where
they're most vulnerable, a good housekeeper can determine mood,
temperament, and daily rhythms. A veteran can tell you "stuff" about
yourself that you'd like to ignore. For a good domestic employee can
sense what's unsaid and hear what's not being talked about!

Blanche White is an amateur detective. She's also a quick study
in the habit of reading people and places. She has an intense spiritual awareness and seeks the guidance of the elders in all things. She
will light a candle, whisper a prayer, hum a tune, and reach a valid
conclusion without missing a beat. Ms. Blanche handles racism,
classism, ageism, ignorance, and homophobia in this series. She also
tackles our inner circle mess of light skin and "good" hair.

Blanche is "real people." She gave me much insight into our
young sister who is serving Mrs. Commander. Young, without family,
in a foreign land, uneducated, and a domestic employee, this child
had a right to be real angry. Since domestics are assumed to be "things
and objects," most people talk openly around them, for they work
silently, unobserved and nonintrusive. House workers are not thought
to be very intelligent nor looked to for the value of their wisdom.

Now let me hurry to say that "house workers" have been raised
in esteem with the Daughters of the American Republic wanting to
erect a statue of "Mammy" in Washington, D.C.! For the realization
came to them that "Mammy" had provided the love, nurture, and
guidance in many homes that "pedestal-placed moms" could not.
Yet always remember that "Mammy" was heavy of figure, dark of

skin, and older. She wore a head rag to hide her "heathen" hair and kept a perpetual smile on her plump-cheeked face. "Mammy" was a serious "caricature" of a black domestic worker as she dispensed wisdom, care, and good food.

Our Lil' Sista doesn't fit this image. She was a mere child. Yet she seems to have made a place for herself in the home of Commander and Mrs. Naaman. For the Bible says, "she served." Perhaps she worked to keep her mind occupied. Maybe she was simply industrious by nature and ethnic origin. I can imagine that she'd seen her family killed by Aramean soldiers and felt fortunate to be alive. Whatever her inner motivation, it's obvious that she made an impact upon the storyteller, for the canon records her position and work ethic.

She understood the value of making herself necessary to the place where she was forced to be at the time. Since we don't know her age, just that she's a young Israelite girl, we know she wasn't educated by formal schooling. For only males were sent to schools in order to become leaders in later life. Yet we discover that our young sister had wisdom beyond her years. She'd picked up the skill of acute listening and storing information. She'd discovered a household secret—her male enslaver had been caught captive to the disease of leprosy.

He was a "big man" in Aram. He was respected for his leadership abilities. He had a wonderful future ahead until leprosy entered the picture of his life. In a few days he would be forced to leave his family and make his home in the leper colony outside of town. In a few days his uniform and status would become meaningless as he would be exiled, forced to yell out, "I'm unclean" to any one approaching him. In a few days he would find himself exiled from his home, forced to live among strangers. In a few days he would personally come to discover the inner thought life and lonely feelings of Lil' Sista. How ironic.

I would have said "Goody, goody gumdrops!" I would have thought it was his just due. I would have been glad to see my enslaver get the punishment of a long and slow death sentence. I would have kept my mouth shut, done my job, and been waiting for the day he was forced out of his home and away from his family. It's a good thing I wasn't Lil' Sista! She teaches me a better way. For she shared what she knew with the enemy! She told Naman's wife about a prophet in Israel who could heal.

Some of the most reassuring words in the Christian Bible are found in Gen 22:1: "And it came to pass" (or "Sometime later"), which implies that things will happen, situations will occur, circumstances do crop up, but time passes and life goes on. Whatever situation you are in today does not have "the end" attached to it! God has a new scene prepared. God has a different stage set. God has an entirely different production prepared for your arrival. For "some time later," things won't be the same!

This little girl was the instigator of a miracle! Her testimony was heard and believed because she had been serious about doing her best in a hostile situation. I wish I had thought of the Ten Commandments for Working in a Hostile Environment. I wish I had learned them many years and several hostile places back! Bishop T. D. Jakes is the originator of these Ten Commandments. I copied them as he preached on television one Sunday morning. They are worth sharing with you, my sista.

1) Understand that God anoints you for trouble. Be sure you are a Christian and put on the whole armor of God before going to work.

2) Don't expect to be appreciated on your job. Only expect a paycheck. Don't look to work places for affirmation and personal relationships.

3) Do your job well, but always remember your mission. God put you there to be a light!

4) Seek opportunities to change the atmosphere without commenting on the problems. When you talk, make it a conversation with God, in prayer.

5) Don't allow the environment to get inside of you. You should influence it. You are sent to give and not to receive!

6) Increase your capacity to work with different personalities. God will often bless you through people you don't even like!

7) Remember that where you are does not define where you are going. Keep in mind that God has the plan for your life! This will deliver you from frustration.

8) Get the optimum results with minimal confusion. Be effective without adding to the problem.

9) Don't be associated with any one of the groups or cliques. Labels will limit your usefulness to God. Work with everyone, but be labeled by no one. And remember, God has given you more than one gift. Use each gift as a different source of revenue and don't be limited to just the salary from where you work.

10) Always keep a song (psalm) near you. Hold onto your praise. Keep a consecrated place within that is reserved only for God!

This young woman had not been to a "Woman Thou Art Loosed" conference, but she sure had an effective plan for making God look good. If only you and I were as wise with the age we have attained!

WOMAN WISDOM SPEAKS: "Keep my words, and treasure my commands within you. Keep my commands and live, and my law as the apple of your eye. Bind them on your fingers; write them on the tablet of your heart. Say to wisdom, 'You are my sister,' and call understanding your nearest kin" (Prov. 7:1–40).

WOMANIST WISDOM SAYS: Whatever our profession, it is honorable and useful for making God look good!

A BODACIOUS WOMAN would make a banner out of the Ten Commandments for Working in a Hostile Environment. She would paste them on her bathroom mirror. She would tape them to her desk. She would memorize them and repeat them to herself as she rides or drives or walks to work. She would make them her mantra and say them even as she prays! For words to the wise are sufficient . . . or so they say!

9

AND HANNAH ROSE!

1 Samuel 1:1–28

I enjoy a good love story. There is nothing better than sitting down reading a good book where love conquers all. I like a story where there are challenges, hurdles to overcome, and obstacles to be removed, and in which a good woman wins in the end. I remember when the sequel to *Gone with the Wind* came out. It was entitled simply *Scarlett*. I don't like books about the Civil War where the slaves are happy, the plantation is a resort, and everybody lives happily ever after. So when *Scarlett* came out I had no intention to pay money for it. I put my name on the waiting list at the public library. It took almost two months after its release for the librarian to call me.

I remember it as if it were yesterday. I went to the library and picked up the book. Then I went home, made myself a cup of tea, went upstairs to the TV room, sat in the recliner, and opened the book while all the family was out. I read the first line and closed the book. Got up, returned the book to the library, and went to the local bookstore to purchase my own. The first line grabbed my attention. The first sentence allowed me to know that the Scarlett of *Gone with the Wind* had changed, grown up, been transformed, and was a woman with a mission in life.

Do you want to know what the first sentence says? It reads, "This will soon be over and then I can go home to Tara." She was standing at the gravesite of her best friend. She wanted to weep, to wail, and to fall into a swoon familiar to southern, fragile white women. But she stood there. She talked to herself. She decided that there was another option to falling down, acting helpless, and being out of control. She comforted herself with the promise that better things are ahead. She rationalized that there was a new tomorrow on the other side of her painful reality. She understood that the graveyard was "the end" for Melly, but not for her.

Scarlett got into her carriage and, due to the ruts of the road, she fell to the floor, hitting her elbow on the window frame. When she got up there was a sharp pain running up and down her arm. She didn't cry out. She didn't stop Elias, the driver. Instead she talked to herself and said, "It's only physical pain. I can stand this." It was the other pain, the postponed, delayed, denied, shadowy pain that she couldn't bear. Not yet, not here, not when she was all alone. She had to get to Tara. Mammy was there. Mammy would hold her, love her, would share her pain and help her to bear it.

She got up ready to go to find the help she needed. Mammy was not the slave who had raised her and nurtured her as a child. Mammy was not the cook and housekeeper for the family. To Scarlett, Mammy was her Christ figure. Mammy knew her at her worst and accepted her for who she was. Scarlett wanted to get home to love.

Life is about getting up and going to get help. Life is not fair. Life is not pretty. Life is not always wonderful, smooth, and without bumps. But we have to know how to get up. We have to remember that there is One who loves us, who cares for us, who cheerleads for us, who intercedes for us, and who has given his life for us. This One has shown us how to keep getting up. For we are an Easter people, and getting up is our theme song.

This means that we need to expect, anticipate, and be fully prepared for being knocked down, struck down, talked down, pushed down, and even held down. But our faith says that this will soon be over and we will get up. There is a biblical example of a woman who knew about getting up when life tried to hold her down. Hannah is another woman who declared, "This will soon be over." And she kept on getting up.

The book of Samuel is the story of God's love for the people of Israel. There are two books that contain the story of the Christ figure Samuel, who was a dream in his mother's heart. The history of the last two judges, Eli and Samuel, are contained in these books. The history of the first and second kings, Saul and David, are written in these books. This story details how Eli, the high priest, allowed his sons to bring him to ruin and how the glory of God left the people of Israel. This work tells the world about a mother who prayed and a God who listened to her prayers. Her son, Samuel, became the first priest-prophet-judge who anointed and counseled the people of God. It all happened because Sister Hannah kept telling herself, "This will soon be over and then I can . . ."

Hannah was a wife who was dearly loved. Her husband, Elkanah, was a Levite (a priest), but one who lived in the country. So he did not have to go into the temple at Shiloh to worship and to sacrifice. But he was a devout man who had a generous heart, and in honor of all God had blessed him with he wanted to offer his own sacrifice. On the day of sacrifice, because he was a Levite and entitled to the provisions of the temple, he gave portions of what was brought to his family. However, he gave Hannah a double portion, because he loved her (1 Sam. 1:1–28).

Talk about a divided family. Talk about mess in the house. Talk about a family where there was dysfunction—it's right here in this scripture. The original cause of this love triangle came about when Elkanah transgressed the original institution of marriage. For Jesus says that the law permitted divorce, but "from the beginning, it was not to be so" (Matt. 25:5–8). Elkanah married Hannah and loved her. But she could have no children—"The Lord closed her womb" (1 Sam. 1:6). Because a man wants sons, Elkanah decided to marry a more fertile woman, Peninnah. She had children and she had attitude. She provoked Hannah severely. She irritated her on purpose. She mocked her empty womb. She made fun of her barrenness. And this went on year after year. Whenever Hannah went up to the house of God, Peninnah messed with her mind.

Both women were blessed. Hannah was blessed with a husband who loved her more than ten sons. Peninnah was blessed to be fruitful and had a house full of children, both sons and daughters. They were women of different temperaments. Peninnah had the babies, but not her husband's love. She grew haughty and evil. She couldn't find it in her heart to be thankful or grateful. On the other hand, Hannah had love but wanted children. So she went into distress and grew melancholy and discouraged. She would not eat. She was sad. Bitter tears became her daily prayers. They could have both stayed in the shape they were in, but Hannah rose.

Verse 9 says that "after they had eaten and drunk at Shiloh, the place of the temple, Hannah rose and presented herself before God." Principle number one says that if you want to keep getting up, keep on going to worship. When you can't sing, let others sing for you. When you can't pray, let others pray for you. When you don't have anything to give, others have given through the years on your behalf. Whatever you do when distress comes to visit you, don't stop presenting yourself before God.

Verse 9 also tells us to be careful how we act, judge, speak, and discern when we say that we are the Church. Our job is to bring others to Christ, and people will come when we invite them. It is our job not to look down our noses at them when they arrive! For Eli represents the Church. He was sitting at the doorpost of the temple. Have you ever heard of the term "gatekeeper"?

There are always those among us who feel it is their job, their role, their task to save the Church from those they feel don't quite measure up. There are those among us who feel that it is their job, their role, their task to protect God's Church. Honestly, we are only stewards. We don't have a Church. The building where we worship is not the Church anyway! The people who have Christ in their hearts are the Church, when they gather anywhere!

God really does know how to protect the Church. God even knows how to maintain and upkeep physical structures. For it was God's plan and design that set forth the details of every Christian sanctuary. The plan was given to Moses by God. So gatekeepers may be in place, but they don't work for God!

Hannah, our sister, was in deep distress. She was praying to God and weeping every word. God reads tears like spoken prayers. She made a vow to God for a child. She promised that she would sacrifice her child in service to God for all of his life. She just wanted to bear him. In verse 12, the gatekeeper thought she was drunk. Wonderful, discerning, caring person that he was, he attacked the sister who was in distress. "How long will you make a drunken spectacle of yourself. Put away your wine." He made an assumption. He passed judgment. He pronounced his verdict. He thought he was the gatekeeper for God's Church. Principle number two is that God does not employ gatekeepers. God sent Jesus to teach us how to open wide the gates and invite whosoever will to come right on inside.

I've had this Hannah experience with the Church. If you are honest, so have you. People have made assumptions. People have passed judgments. People have pronounced verdicts. People have made serious attempts to be gatekeepers for God. And like Eli they have been misinformed. Yes, well-intentioned. But truly misinformed. We have lived this passage in our local congregations. I am grateful that the gatekeeper, Brother Eli, did not have the final word. For the story does not end there. It goes on to say that Hannah set the record straight. She told her side of the story.

She tells our side of the story as she asserts in verse 15, "I am a woman deeply troubled, but I have done no wrong. I am not a drunk. I am not a worthless woman. I am pouring out my soul before God." Brother Gatekeeper had to back up and give her a divine benediction. "Go in peace; the God of Israel grant your petition."

When she heard the divine benediction, Hannah rose, went home, and left her sadness by the wayside. A change came over her. Transformation took place within her. She was not the same any longer. For the scripture says, "They rose early in the morning, and worshiped before God" (1 Sam. 1:19). When they went home, Sister got pregnant, for God remembered her.

Principle number three is the most difficult to do. For it says that when you are feeling your worst, when you have been knocked down hard, when it feels as if you can't win for losing, get up and keep on moving toward God. When you get up and move to worship, bring the sacrifice of praise. For whining does not influence

God. Complaining does not get God's attention. Fussing and cussing won't persuade the Ancient of Days to come quickly to your aid. But when we decide to worship God in spirit and in truth, God will come to our aid.

This story is here for you, my Sista, to get up. If you are one sitting on the sidelines waiting for everything to be smooth and wonderful before you decide to stick and to stay, God is calling you to get up.

If you are one who has been half-stepping, sometimes in and sometimes out, not serious about the ministry God has called you to do, God is calling again, get up.

If you have been cheating on God, thinking this was a graveyard, where we are to minister to the ancient fossils of history and to worship antique dead yesterdays, God is calling loudly and clearly, get up.

If you are waiting for the return of long ago, when the Church was full, the choir was full, the members were vital, and involved, and the offerings were more than enough to do what needed to be done, then this is God's call for you to get up. For if we invite them, they will come. If we give our whole selves, the realm of Christ will grow. And if we offer unto God our reasonable service, souls will be added to the kingdom and God will be glorified.

Today I can say to Church folks, thanks for talking about me. Thanks for lying about me. Thanks for passing false rumors and empty innuendos about me. For it has made me more determined to keep on getting up. I know that God is in the blessing business and I am surely in line for multiple blessings. The Word declares, "Blessed are you when people revile you, curse you and say all manner of evil against you falsely for my sake." This is the promise of the Beatitudes.

Wherever we are today is only a season of transition. And transitions are temporary. They come to pass. So, like Scarlett, I am persuaded that "this will soon be over and then I can . . ." do whatever task God has sent me to do. And, my sista, so can you!

God knows why you chose to read this story at this particular time. God knew what would be erected to block your forward movement to advance the realm of God. So this day, this hour, God is calling you and me loudly and clearly. Whatever our excuse has been, it's time to get up.

Would you please repeat after me: "This will soon be over." What do you need to be finished, to be over, to be done with so you can get it right with God, with yourself, and with your neighbor? You fill in the blanks.

Now, the second part of the prayer is this (please, repeat it after me): "This will soon be over and, then I can . . ." What is God calling you to do this day and this hour? You fill in the blanks.

The place where you are right now is your altar. The throne room of glory is open to assist you in being all you can be for God. You just have to decide to do like Hannah and get up! Thanks be unto God for the victory of a second, a third, a fourth . . . chance.

WOMAN WISDOM SPEAKS: "I, wisdom, dwell with prudence, and find out knowledge and discretion. The reverence of God is to hate evil; pride and arrogance and the evil way and the perverse mouth I hate. Counsel is mine, and sound wisdom; I am understanding, I have strength" (Prov. 8:12–14).

WOMANIST WISDOM SAYS: Bust a move, Sista! There is a time for prayer and discernment. There is a time for consultation and networking. And there is a time to rise up and get to stepping toward your greatness. If you make one step, God will make two! Is there a twitch in your foot?

A BODACIOUS WOMAN would understand that her life is not bound by what "the people" say but what the Word of God has promised. Put on your best clothes. Pick out your best pair of shoes and go bodaciously about your business of strutting your stuff, Ms. Hannah!

10

A NECESSARY AFFAIR

John 4

"*O*nce upon a time" begins a story. "Once upon a time" says that in history there was a teachable moment. Someone learned something. Some insight was gained. It happened not today, but "once upon a time." Whether we want to tell it or not, we all have a "once upon a time" story to tell. For there was a time when we were not sitting in worship, singing praise, carrying our Bibles, and preparing to take Communion. "Once upon a time" we were out of relationship with God, wanted nothing to do with Jesus, and had little patience for folks who wanted to talk to us about holiness and salvation. That was us, "once upon a time."

Thank God for Jesus, who chased us down, found us at our worst, hung around with us in our sin, saw what we were, and loved us enough to have a necessary affair with us. For the real deal is that Jesus has a history of going to the edges, searching for those on the margins of life, and engaging them in necessary affairs. "Once upon a time," on the edge of Samaria, by the side of an old well, Jesus deliberately stopped to transform an unnamed, foreign woman's life. She is my testimony. And this story is my story. It's a divine encounter worth taking another look at as we prepare to become our very best selves.

The story is found in the fourth chapter of the Gospel of John, verses 4–15 as we begin. John wrote a universal message to help us see that Jesus is the Savior of the whole wide world and not just of the Jews. John dwells on the message that God so loved the world — not just the church, not just the righteous, not just the dutiful, but the world. God so loved the world that Jesus was given as our perfect sacrifice. It's in that context that we find Jesus, weary from battling with the Jewish religious folks and headed for Galilee. But the text tells us that before he can go to do further ministry among his own in order to face Calvary, he has to have a necessary affair with this woman.

My story began one night in my hometown of Gary, Indiana. I was young, shapely, fine, fast, and employed. I was on the prowl every Friday night. I was divorced, had my own car, had two sons, and had moved in with my grandparents for their childcare benefits as I worked and ran the streets. Every Friday, I could be found at the Sportsman Bar and Bowling Alley.

The Sportsman had a fine bartender whose name was Fred. He was tall, yellow, had sandy hair, and was good looking. He never had acted in any manner but friendly with me. But I had my eye on Fred. Every Friday I would be in Sportsman with my crew, styling and profiling.

This particular Friday, it was snowing like crazy. As a matter of fact, a blizzard had been forecast. But weather wasn't going to stop me. I put the boys to bed and started getting dressed to go to the Sportsman. My Granddad was a man of very few words. And he surely had never spoken harshly to me. I was the apple of his eye. But, with a blizzard on the way, Big Daddy stopped by my bedroom.

He questioned my good sense about going out in a snowstorm. I told him I had to go. He shook his head and said, "You might go, but you won't be driving a car tonight." It shocked me. I'd never seen this side of my Grandfather. And Grandmother, conveniently in their room, didn't come to my aid. So, I called a cab. For my crew was waiting. Fred was waiting. I wasn't going to miss the party.

Of course, it took a couple of hours for a cab to get to our house in that weather. I can't describe how the cab driver looked at me when I gave him my destination. We slipped and slid, got stuck, and stopped. But he took me to the Sportsman. I was surprised to see so few cars when we arrived. I knew my crew was waiting on me. I was shocked as I walked in the door, with my coat opened so the gang could see my cute little mini dress and plastic go-go boots to match.

There was no one in the bar but Fred. God knows that was good enough for me. He was just the man I wanted to see. As I was taking off my coat, with a big smile on my face, Fred looked up and asked, "Linda, what in the world are you doing here in this storm?" Before I could answer, he continued.

Do you want to know what Fred said to me? He said, "Don't take off your coat; I'm closing up and I'll take you home!" And he did. There was no crew. There was no party. And there was no affair that night. I was taken home with my eyes wide opened. That was a teachable moment for me.

Once upon a time, Big Daddy and Fred taught me lessons I have never forgotten. I learned that the hole in my soul could not be filled by men. I discovered that something was missing in my life that left a void that I was trying to satisfy in all the wrong ways. The crew didn't meet my needs. Going out partying didn't meet my needs. There was no man who could satisfy the inner longing in my spirit. There was no drink, no dance, no sex that could make me feel whole, fulfilled, or complete. I was searching. I was seeking. I was looking. I was trying. But the answer was not outside of me. The answer was inside of me.

Jesus was waiting all the time for me to wake up, to come to myself, and to discover that every heart, every soul, and every spirit is empty until it's found its home in Christ. And Jesus was there all the time! Jesus was waiting patiently in line, until I was willing to allow that spiritual and eternal satisfaction to spring up from a well that was lying dormant and untapped within me.

What we have to understand is that the Bible does not just speak to us. The Bible speaks about us. This woman, this unnamed sister, the unnamed foreign and ignored female, tells many of our stories. But, as a central character in the book of life, she stands in for every brother too. For the reality is that all of us have to have an affair with the only One who satisfies the longing soul. John is so precise as he says Jesus had to go through Samaria.

There were other ways to Galilee. Most self-respecting Jews would not go through Samaria because Samaritans were considered heathens who had walked away from the pure Jewish faith. They had allowed intermarriage with some of the Jews' worst enemies, the Assyrians. So "pure" Jews would walk seventeen miles out of the way to avoid Samaria. Jesus, however, leaves the Jewish Church folks to go and have a necessary affair with a foreign woman who doesn't feel that she has any need for him.

In this story, Jesus becomes me, hungry for a necessary affair. And Girlfriend's name is "Fred"! For she honestly didn't want to be bothered!

Now, one thing I love about the Bible is that it tells the truth on everybody. In the text we see a comment that allows the reader to get a clue about the background that's going on in the story. We discover in verse 7 that the male disciples have been sent on an errand to buy food. When life is too much for me to handle, I go and get my nails done.

I remember the day we discovered that our daughter, who was on her way back to the University of New Mexico, was pregnant. After I told Mista Chuck what I had learned, I went to get my nails done. It was a maneuver to delay my having to deal with our daughter face to face. We all have our individual avoidance mechanisms. One of mine is my nails. The other is to run to the malls!

The boys couldn't handle what Jesus was about to do, which was to break down barriers, go against traditions, establish new guidelines about who is in the Church and who is not, so, due to their not being able to handle the implications of this necessary affair, the boys were sent to the mall to shop for lunch.

In John 4:6–21, most folks want to deal with the history of this woman. There are forty-two verses dedicated to this necessary affair. Only three are about her interactions with her spouses and the man she was living with then. We have to consider many things as we look at these three verses.

First, the woman did not have the privilege of choosing a man. This is not a twenty-first-century story. In the day of Jesus, marriage arrangers made deals between parents. The bride's family had to pay for some male to take the daughter. Folks, understand that when male children were born, men celebrated. When female children were born, men wept.

Today, in our modern times, an Orthodox Jew worships the same way and uses the same prayer that was used in the days of Moses. It is prayed three times daily: "God, I thank you that I am not a heathen" (a nonbeliever). "God, I thank you that I am not a gentile" (a non-Jew). "God, I thank you that I am not a woman" (a nonmale).

So, we have to consider how this woman was treated by her family if five times they have had to pay for her marriage. Would that leave a hole in her soul?

In addition, the tradition demanded that if a woman married into a family she remained in that family. If her spouse died, she was passed on to another brother in the family. Remember the story of Tamar, who was married to two brothers, Ur and Onan, and was refused the third one, Shelah, by Judah, their father? So what if this woman, or you, had to marry five of your brothers-in-law? Would that leave a hole in your soul?

I submit to you that a primary reason Jesus had to go to Samaria was to minister to the hole in this sister's soul. Rejection leaves a big hole. Abandonment leaves a big hole. When a man wanted to divorce a woman, all he had to do was go to the elders at the gate, file his complaint, go back to the tent door, face the east, and declare three times, "I divorce you. I divorce you. I divorce you." And the marriage was over. The woman was sent home in disgrace if there was no other brother to pass her on to. Being passed along like a piece of furniture leaves a big hole. The woman was empty. The woman was hurting. The woman needed something within!

So Jesus and the woman had a long conversation about her giving him a drink of water. You simply need to recall the details of how water has always figured in God's plans for our salvation. For 70 percent of the known world is water. Our bodies are composed of 70 percent water. You can go for days without eating, but within three or four days without water, every system will shut down, for we cannot exist without water. We begin our life journey in an embryonic sac of waters. The Exodus centered around a great body of water known as the Red Sea. In the wilderness of sin, Moses struck a rock, and fresh, living water begin to flow for the people of God.

Go back and read the Old Testament stories and get a glimpse of the love affairs that center around water. In Genesis 24:10–16, 30;

Genesis 29:4–12; and Exodus 2:15–21, three stories of necessary affairs at wells are told. In the first story, Abraham sends a servant to find a wife for his son, Isaac. Rebekah is found at a well. In the second story, when Jacob runs away to his uncle Laban's, he finds the love of his life, Rachel, at a well. Finally, in story number three, when Moses, trying to hide away from the Pharaoh in the desert, saves seven sisters, the daughters of the high priest, he meets his wife, Zipporah, at a well. Each story is a love affair that points us toward this necessary affair in John 4.

We are people of water. Remember the Middle Passage, the great Mississippi River, and the waters of our baptisms. Water—we drink it, wash in it, clean with it, and play in it, for it is essential. God has always had love affairs begin around water. Isaac, Jacob, and Moses are all symbols and types of the coming Savior. As they met women at old wells, they show us the significance of Jesus having a necessary affair with an unnamed woman at Jacob's well. This is the longest recorded dialogue in scripture. Jesus and this woman talk about many issues of life.

Jesus and this hurting woman talk about theology—who God really is to the world. They talk about our internal needs of living water. They talk about her wounded spirit. They talk about what true worship will be in the future. And they talk about him being the expected Messiah.

Jesus spends a long and intense period of time in dialogue with an unnamed, foreign woman who is hurting and in isolation from her community. He meets her on the edge of her existence, on the edge of town, where they can have quality time alone. There Jesus broke down the barriers to true relationship. He broke down the barriers between males and females. He broke down the barriers of who was in and who was out of the Church. He broke down the barriers of what seemed to be her reality—being alone, rejected, abandoned, and unworthy—by showing her that she deserved to be treated with dignity, acceptance, and respect. Jesus broke down the barrier between our need for physical food and spiritual food. For when the disciples came back with a physical meal from "the mall," Jesus told them that he had already eaten with the woman! "I have food that you know nothing about" (John 4:32).

The woman's life was changed. Her thinking was challenged. Her world turned upside down. This necessary affair with Jesus gave her new hope, a new outlook on life, and a new day to make a different kind of history. This new history would change others' lives. On that day, in that place, there was a necessary healing for the woman, who became a necessary witness for Jesus. This same formerly rejected woman ran into town and witnessed to the very ones who had hurt her and made her a marginalized person in the past.

There were many necessary elements in this necessary affair at the well that day. Both Jesus and the woman had to make this journey. She had to go for water and Jesus had to meet her there. They both asked necessary questions. "Give me water," they requested of each other.

They both made necessary challenges. "Are you greater than Jacob, our father?" she asked. "Woman, go call your husband," Jesus responded.

They both met the necessary requirements for true salvation. Jesus offered it. The woman accepted it.

They both made necessary revelations. "I have no husband," said the woman. "I am the Messiah," declared Jesus.

They both made necessary requests. "Do me a favor," they asked each other.

And they both received necessary blessings. The hole in the woman's soul was filled. Jesus got a gentile harvest out of the deal! As a matter of fact, an entire town got blessed because of this necessary affair! (John 4:40).

What we miss in this text is the reality that Jesus asked this woman to do him a favor by giving him a drink of water. When he asked for the water, and she responded, even after all her questions and smart answers, the law of reciprocity went into effect. The law of reciprocity says that you will reap what you sow. But when it comes to God, you can't beat God giving. So when she did Jesus a favor with well water, he was obligated to offer her a greater gift of living water.

When she did that small act of kindness for Jesus, a necessary healing was effected for her and she became a necessary witness for both the power and the reality of the Messiah.

Today we are offered this same living water that will spring up afresh within us and make us whole regardless of the situations that we face in life. We, who are called by the name of Christ, are obligated to return the favor by working for the salvation for others.

In Matthew 25, Jesus says that those who will sit on God's right side in eternity are those who in this life will go to the edges and feed the hungry, visit the sick, infirm, and institutionalized, clothe the naked, and care for God's neglected and tossed-aside little ones.

For on the edges and fringes of life are those who are not just physically hungry, but those starving for meaning to their life. There are those whose lives are parched dry because they have tried everything else but have never experienced a necessary affair with Jesus Christ. They do like I did and seek for love in all the wrong places. On the edges, there are those who not only need clothing for their body, but whose lives are naked and not covered with honor, character, or integrity.

We are not simply to go to the jails and prisons. There are too many who are walking around our communities who need us to show them a way out of their destructive and dehumanizing dependencies. There are social structures that severely limit our freedom of creativity. Not only are we to minister to the sick and shut in, but to those who are locked into racist bigotry and intolerance for those with different beliefs or darker skins. Too many people are living with all types of inner alienation, which keeps them locked away from the love to be found in true Christian community. We are the ones who have to do Jesus the favor of going there . . . doing that . . . introducing them to the living water!

Jesus has a need to meet with each of us! It's a divine necessity! This woman at the well is each one of us. She has no name, so each one of us is her. We all need Jesus in order to be whole and complete. And, whatever and wherever our well may be, he will meet us there to make us whole. If your well is sex, alcohol, drugs, gambling, overeating, hanging out, low self-esteem, talking about others to make yourself feel better, lying in order to build up others' image of you, or simply relying on your job title or position to feed that inner need—no matter where you are today, Jesus yearns to have a necessary affair with you!

Living water is available. Living water can be drawn upon. Living water can be accessed wherever we may be. Living water is provided to us, in the form of a cup of juice and a piece of bread. Living water is available to us in the form of prayer support and that still, inner peace that comes our way. Living water is available to us in the comforting words of scriptures that heal our wounded souls. And living water is available to us in the community of believers where we are viable parts of the Body.

With a confession of sin, repentance of past behaviors, and a willingness to ask the Savior to help us, Jesus will meet us and ask us to do him a small favor. Just meet with him. He will be there in order to fulfill our deepest, unspoken needs. He will meet us and provide the answer to our most perplexing questions. He will meet with us to be in a love relationship with us. He will meet us to become our Living Water and our Bread for the journey. He longs to meet with us, to refresh us, to restore us, and to make us brand new!

The need to meet with us and to change our old history and allow us to make new beginnings is an imperative with Jesus Christ. He has already made all the necessary arrangements to have a love affair with us. On the night of his betrayal, he became a mother to his friends. He invited them to dinner. He put on his apron. He served bread baked by women and wine pressed by their feet. But before he served them, he washed their feet. He bathed them, cleansed them, and got them ready for this very necessary meal.

It was only after getting them ready that he took off his apron and went to the head of the table and stood as the father image to the household. He became the host of the meal. For the meal that we eat is called the Lord's Supper. We don't invite ourselves. We are invited by Jesus Christ himself.

On that night, he took the bread and he blessed it and gave God thanks for it. For he had seen his mother, watched both Mary and Martha, along with many other women, go out into the fields of wheat and harvest lonely, single stalks into bundles. He had seen them break it down into usable parts and grind what was edible into grain. He knew how they took that grain, mixed it with a bit of yeast, salt, and milk and made bread, which was the stable of every family. Jesus had seen women roll that mixture and shape it, and put it into the fire to bake. So Jesus thanked God for the community of elements that became bread to feed the world. He broke the bread and gave it unto his friends, his followers, his disciples, and they ate together.

Following the meal, he took the cup of wine, which had begun as solo pieces of grapes, grown under the boiling sun. As the women gathered the clusters, washed them, and took them down to the wine press, there they took off their sandals and smashed the juices from the peels to make a drink that satisfied when the water and yeast had fermented together. Jesus gave God thanks for the community of elements that served to become wine and slake their thirst. Then he passed a common cup to his friends, his followers, his disciples. And they drank together.

This has become an essential and necessary meal. For Jesus told them that every time they ate it to do it and remember his necessary visit upon the earth. And every time they drank the juice it became the blood of the New Covenant he was making with all the people of God.

This necessary meal became a symbol of the eternal banquet that is to come. But the meal didn't stop there, for he went on to Calvary, where he met needs there by becoming the meal. He stopped dying to take care of his mother. He stopped dying to take a thief into the realm of God.

He stopped dying to say, "I'm thirsty," so that he could allow those who were crucifying him to do him a favor and put the law of reciprocity into effect for all times and for you and for me. For when they lifted that bitter cup to his mouth, he said to a sin-filled world, "If you keep up my mission, I'll help you in every time of need. I'll never leave you and I'll never forsake you. If you care for my people, I'll bless you and sustain you. If you give yourself for others, I will take care of you. If you will attend to the needs of the world, I will feed you so that you will never hunger. And I'll satisfy you with water that will spring up inside of you as a living well."

All we have to say is, "Fill my cup; I lift it up; come and quench this thirsting of my soul. Bread of heaven, feed me 'til I want no more. Here's my cup. Fill it up. Only you Jesus can make me whole."[1] But Jesus didn't stop there!

For he became the body broken and the blood poured out. When they stuck him in the side and the blood and the water poured forth, they ran down the cross and kissed at the bottom of a symbol of sin and shame. As those elements met in a necessary affair, the Church of the Living God was born!

I'm so glad that Jesus was waiting for me that night at the Sportsman when I discovered that Fred and my crew were not the answer, and I had to turn to the Living Water. In the midst of a blizzard, Jesus was there all the time. He didn't take a cab. He didn't slip and slide, but he was waiting there all the time.

Wherever you are, Jesus is there waiting. For he wants you, like that nameless woman and like me, to become a witness to those who have been watching your foolish search.

The woman left her water pot. She ran back and said, "Come see a man who has put my and your business in the street." The Bible says that many from that town came and that Jesus stayed in Samaria for two days. History was made. Many were converted. The male disciples didn't do it. The Apostle Paul wasn't on the scene. The first witness and evangelist to the gentiles was a rejected, abandoned, foreign woman who had a necessary affair with Jesus! Thanks be unto God, this same opportunity is ours!

WOMAN WISDOM SPEAKS: "Wisdom has built her house, she cries out from the highest places of the city, 'Whoever is simple, let that one turn in here!' To the one who lacks understanding, she says, 'Come, eat of my bread and drink of the wine I have mixed. Forsake foolishness and live, go in the way of understanding'" (Prov. 9:1, 4–6).

WOMANIST WISDOM SAYS: Jesus might be my man, but he will stop by your house for a necessary affair! And it's all good!

A BODACIOUS WOMAN would ensure that she's with the right man! For all that shines is not gold! All who look good on the outside don't have "do right" on the inside. It's alright that you have made mistakes in the past as you kissed frogs, seeking the prince, but to continue with this behavior is ludicrous! For a worthless man cannot turn into your Prince Charming! You have to look beyond the exterior and be prepared to change *you*, before the assortment of frogs stop coming your way. When you have had a necessary affair with Jesus, you become different. You become new. This is when you begin to spray on "frog repellant"! Now, you are prepared to make a new history and to write a different story with your life.

11

GOD OF A SECOND CHANCE

Mark 5

*I*n his book *Who Moved My Cheese?* Dr. Spencer Johnson
does an excellent job of creating a story about two little
creatures, Sniff and Scurry living in a maze with two little people named Hem and Haw. All of them were tiny.
All of them foraged for food each day. All of them had jogging suits
and gym shoes. As fate would have it, all of them discovered a huge
supply of cheese at Station L.

Sniff and Scurry were not gifted with intellect like the little people.
They were simple creatures who just had survival instinct. So even
though they were satisfied eating the cheese at Station L, they kept
their jogging suits on and tied their gym shoes around their necks.

Now the little people took off their gym shoes, lost them, and
threw away their jogging suits. They got satisfied. They became con-
tent. They got fat and lazy. They built themselves homes right outside
of Station L. They begin to sing with gusto, "I shall not be moved!"

But one day when Sniff and Scurry and the little people arrived
at Station L, they all noticed that the cheese was in short supply.
What was left was smelling and had mold on it. They all ate. But
Sniff and Scurry fastened up their jogging suits and put on their gym

shoes. Sniff said, "I'm going out to scout for more cheese." Scurry said, "When you smell it, I'll run and find it." So the two creatures with survival in mind took off and left Station L.

The following dialogue took place then between the two little people. One said, "We need to hunt up our gym shoes and jogging suits." The other said, "I shall not be moved." The first one said, "The cheese is gone." The other one said, "They will bring it back." The first one questioned, "Why didn't we notice that the supply was dwindling?" The other one declared, "They owe us some new cheese." So the little people sat there, starving to death, debating the issue of who, where, what, and why. But they made no conscious effort to go and find any new source of cheese!

Finally, one of the little people woke up. The light bulb came on. An "ah ha" moment broke in and the realization hit him that "the cheese is really gone!" Then the dilemma became, "Who moved my cheese?"—the title of this book that was devised as a cute way to help business people move off the dime in these days of downsizing, merging, and outsourcing of jobs. All of us who are employed, in any area of life, need to be like Sniff and Scurry. For the reality is that cheese will move!

The question now is, who moved your cheese?

If the thrill is gone and the relationship is empty, who moved your cheese? If the job no longer satisfies you and it's a burden to go to work each day, who moved your cheese? If the joy has left your life and the laughter inside you has dried up, who moved your cheese? For the stark truth is that cheese is whatever satisfies us, floats our boat, puts a grin on our face, and makes life worth living. So who moved your cheese?

Far too many of us are stuck in ruts, lost in a maze, and held captive to a place long after the cheese is gone. When the cheese has become moldy and the smell is getting stronger, we need to be like Sniff and Scurry—ready to read the handwriting on the wall! For the signs of disappearing cheese are all around us. Where did you say your jogging suit and gym shoes were located? For the Holy Spirit is saying that it's time to get up and to move out of this "cheeseless" place.

The unnamed woman in Mark 5 is one who realized that the cheese of her life was dank, moldy, and in short supply. The woman knew that the thrill for her was long gone! She was out of relationship with her family, with her community, and with her church. For her condition of bleeding for twelve years had kept her a prisoner in her home. When a woman had a menstrual cycle she was banished to her quarters—couldn't cook or clean for others, as she was considered and labeled "impure." For this woman in Mark 5 the impurity was constant. If she touched anyone, was in the vicinity of any male, or even cooked a meal that was eaten by others, they became ritually impure.

In this chapter we also find a little twelve-year-old girl. She's one who has never had the chance to fully live before death has snatched her with its powerful grip. Twelve is a significant number in the Bible. There are twelve tribes of Israel. There were twelve disciples chosen. There are twelve gates to the beautiful city. There were twelve years of a serious illness. And there was a child who was twelve years old and dead. The cheese had run out for both of these unnamed sisters.

But there is good news for every woman who needs liberation. There is good news for every woman who has recognized that her cheese supply has moved. There is good news for every one of us who is ready, willing, and able to hear what the Holy Spirit is shouting so loudly in this passage of scripture. For when Jesus came on the scene, one woman began to behave like Sniff and Scurry. She decided not to simply sit and survive, but to experience abundant living. And the father of the little girl went seeking Jesus to come and raise his daughter from her bed. When Jesus is around, things are bound to change.

I'm always intrigued by the older woman whose doctors had done her no good at all. The community had written her off. Her family is not mentioned, but Girlfriend got up, got encouraged, and got gone! The Bible says she began to talk to herself. Sometimes, this is the only good and positive information you will hear. It's called self-talk! It's talking back to yourself the motivating tapes stored in your spirit. She said, "If I can only touch the hem of his garment, I will be made whole."

She didn't want a T. D. Jakes, "Woman Thou Art Loosed" conference. She didn't need a Joyce Meyers or Juanita Bynum assembly.

She wasn't seeking a one-on-one counseling session with Ms. Clio on the hotline. Nor did she expect to be slapped on the head and slain in the spirit. All she wanted to do was to slip up on Jesus and touch the hem of the Teacher's robe.

A rabbi was identified by the fringes on the bottom of his robe. The fringes signified one in a covenant relationship with God. The fringes represented hope. The fringes told a story of new possibilities. So the woman, who knew that her cheese was almost gone, put on her jogging suit and gym shoes and went in search of the One who was wearing the fringes.

Jesus was ministering to the cheeseless that day. The Bible says that the crowd was large and the needs were great. But Jesus allowed for the various interruptions. On a mission of healing, he allowed Jairus, a gentile, to approach him about his twelve-year-old, dying daughter. Jesus allowed his agenda to be changed as he turned to go home with this grieving dad. For Jesus is the God of a second chance.

On his way to do a good deed, up behind Jesus came this bodacious woman. This nameless sister was a woman who knew that she was out of order. She was fully aware that she was breaking the societal rules. She knew that she was disregarding religious traditions. But she is willing to color outside the lines. She dared to think outside the box. For her cheese was almost gone, and she was on the search for a new supply. She'd heard that Jesus was rumored to be a God of second chances.

She sought and found Jesus. She degraded herself to get to him. On her knees, through the great multitude, pushing and shoving like a sales-crazed woman at a 75 percent-off event, she zoned out all others. Her focus was on Jesus alone. And she made contact. She felt her second chance begin the moment she touched him. For the power left him and flowed into her body. There was at that moment liberation from a twelve-year forced isolation. There was at that moment liberation from her pain. There was at that moment the removal of her stigma and her confinement. There was at that moment liberation from her twelve years of undeserved shame.

Those twelve years indicate that it makes no difference to Jesus Christ whether you have been shackled for a long period of your life or whether you've suffered a hellish situation for all of your life. There is help for you. Jesus wants to intervene. Jesus longs to be touched with all of our infirmities, afflictions, and pains. In the very midst of our brokenness and despair, even in the very face of death, Jesus will interrupt his planned agenda to see to the needs of hurting and dying women.

You may be a young sister bound in a habit, a relationship, or a job that is sucking the life from you. Know that Jesus wants to intervene in your life situation. This is a call for a second chance.

You may be an elder sister who has given a great portion of your life to circumstances that are causing you to feel the drain of your life's energy seeping away, like that woman's issue of blood. When you continue to dishonor yourself in relationships you die slowly, day by day. Jesus wants you to know that there is a new cheese supply for you too.

The older sister in this passage smelled death approaching. She read the handwriting on the wall. She realized that the cheese was moldy and running out. She decided to do something! She made a decision. She made a choice. She had determination. She put forth the necessary effort to get up and go somewhere, seeking something that represented new life. She choose not to die, sitting in the same place, isolated, afraid, and alone. She sought help. She went looking for change. She moved outside of her comfort zone, knowing that she would be talked about, despised, and perhaps even killed for "infecting" so many "pure" males in the community! Yet she acted on her belief that Jesus could offer her a second chance at life. She went in search of it. And she found it.

Far too many of us are trapped in death-producing situations. We are simply waiting to die. We are afraid to risk. We are afraid to venture beyond our comfort zones. We stay silent when we ought to be screaming. We keep smiling when we should be raging. We keep putting up with foolishness that is killing us slowly but surely.

We remain in situations with fools far too long. We allow our kids to kill us with their unchecked selfishness, which we support. We permit our men to use and misuse us when they have not sufficiently loved us or known how to make love to us. We keep sitting, knowing that both the cheese and the thrill is gone! But this bodacious woman of our biblical past teaches us how to get up and bust a move!

It's easy to stay in the maze and die. It's easy to give up and prepare for death. It's easy to feel defeated, depressed, and dejected. It takes wisdom to know that this is not the end. It takes womanist courage to know that there is something better waiting just on the other side of through!

If you've been trapped by the wayside of life—situations, circumstances, and people holding you back as you contend with both conflict and strife—if you feel battered, busted, and broken, Girlfriend, you don't have to stay in the shape you are currently in. For the Potter really does want to put you back together again! There is new life. There is fresh cheese. There is more on the other side of this predicament than you have ever anticipated or expected. For the God of a second chance is here for you, rooting, cheering and waiting for you to get up and move out.

What of the littel girl whose father dared to bother Jesus, to interrupt him? That little girl was raised from the dead! The people around her parents laughed and mocked both her father and Jesus as they approached what they considered to be a cheeseless situation for her. But that little girl came out of the room looking for food. And Jesus commanded the parents not to stand around amazed, but to feed the child! Jesus yearns for us to eat sumptuously from the banquet of life!

Sista Girl, know that you are the primary agenda of Jesus Christ! Regardless of your circumstances, no matter how hopeless life seems today, there is good news for you. Jesus loves little people. He has walked in our shoes. Jesus loves the Sniffs and Scurrys of the world who go seeking new cheese. Jesus even loves the Hems and Haws of the world who remain stuck in their mess. For he died and rose to assure each of us new life, new, fresh cheese, and new opportunities for a second, third, fourth, fifth, sixth, seventh . . . chance!

WOMAN WISDOM SPEAKS: "The reverence of God is the beginning of wisdom, and the knowledge of the Holy One is understanding. For by me your days will be multiplied, and the years of life will be added to you. If you are wise, you are wise for yourself, and if you scoff, you will bear it alone" (Prov. 9:10–12).

WOMANIST WISDOM SAYS: We have faced death so many times until it is not funny! Death is not new to us. We have to die to the old so that the new might be born. We have to die to traditions so that new life might be born. We have to die to yesterday so that tomorrow might be born. We have to die to the young in us so that the middle age might be born. And we will die to the middle age so that the aged sage might be born! Only death prepares the way for new creations, new beginnings, and new births to occur in our life. Death is not the end. So go ahead and die to yesterday and yester-ways! God is yet in the business of raising us to new life!

A BODACIOUS WOMAN would decide just what in life was killing her, sucking the life out of her, weakening her resolve to live the abundant life. Then she would shake the dust off her feet and bid it a fond farewell! She wouldn't know where she was going. She wouldn't know just what she was going to do. But she would trust in the God who had called her to provide direction, provision, counsel, and support! For our extremities are God's opportunities to work on our behalf. Take a step forward and watch for signs of God! Be on the alert, for God is on the move!

12

A WOMAN OF EXCELLENCE

Esther 1

*T*here are times in our lives when we learn valuable lessons quite by accident. Sometimes the very best knowledge comes our way not because of how diligent we have been, not due to our effective scholarship, not even because of our ability to apply reason to our circumstances. There comes a time in our life where it makes no difference who you know, what position you have attained, or where you are economically situated; life will present you with new educational opportunities to show just what you have the power to do.

We tend to believe that the time will arrive when we pretty much have it all together. We like to feel comfortable with our intellect. We want to believe that we have fairly well navigated the school of life. And we have the inclination that there is not a whole lot more to learn—nothing else new to be taught and nobody, anywhere, who can honestly teach us a whole lot more.

What I'm trying to say in a delicate way is that most of us would never say it out loud, but when new information tries to present itself to our fixed patterns of thinking and relating, our little inner voice rushes to assure us that we already know it all.

"Been there, done that. Got the tee shirt" is a saying that had to have been born as one woman tried to provide additional information to another one. For the majority of us are quick to see a sister, size up a sister, make critical judgments about a sister, and write her off before she ever opens her mouth. But a woman of excellence knows that there is more to a situation and to a person than what we can see with our naked eye.

A woman of excellence, one who is confident that the good work begun in her by Jesus Christ is continually being perfected, is willing to be a serious student of every one of life's lessons. A woman of excellence, who is in fellowship with the gospel of Jesus Christ, realizes, understands, and appreciates that she is forever in a posture of being a student and is willing to learn more. A woman of excellence, who wants to abound more and more in the knowledge of Jesus Christ, quickly comes to grips with the reality that we can be taught even when we cannot comprehend life's lesson plan.

Often times, even while we are looking, we are not able to figure out what life is trying to teach us. For the truth is that every day is a school day. Every day is one of education. Every day is one of mastering the lessons presented, figuring out the equations and putting the puzzle pieces together quicker and more efficiently. At the end of every day, we had best try to tally up our score. What did we learn? What did we flunk? What repeat lesson came back to visit us again?

My sisters, God is an excellent instructor. You and I will not receive God's mark of excellence until we are able to effectively show by our lives that the hurdles, challenges, struggles, and disappointments of life can't keep us down and have us always singing the blues. You and I will not achieve God's mark of excellence until we can master the principle of working together in unity and with harmony. This is why Pastor Paul explicates in chapter 4 of Philippians that our ministering sisters, Eudodia and Syntyche, have failed this particular life lesson. Yes! They were women well involved in effective ministry, but they had not met the criteria for excellence.

We are quick to label ourselves "excellent," but the standards by which we label ourselves are most often those standards that we know we can pass. A rating of excellence from God demands more than our small human and personally achievable stamp of approval. God requires more from us than we are ever willing to do on our own.

We don't graduate to excellence in three easy lessons. We don't reach excellence by looking good, attending Sunday worship, holding a church office, being a good giver, and perpetuating mediocrity! Excellence demands personal sacrifice. Excellence requires vision. Excellence mandates risk taking. And excellence dictates that we learn from every painful situation that life presents.

There are times in our lives when we learn valuable lessons after the deed has been done—after we have taken the hit, after we have lost the round, after the romance has died, after the relationship is over, after the fiasco has blown up in our face, and after gallons and gallons of snot and tears! There are some lessons in life that only loss and hindsight can teach us. So this day I want to back us up and have us take another view at the story outlined in the book of Esther.

Yes, it's an old, old story. Yes, it's a common passage to be drug out for Women's Day, Missionary Day, and even for Missions Day. But today I want us to grapple with the woman of excellence whose name is not Esther, but Vashti. Church history has not done this sister justice. Our sermons and talks have not exhausted the multiple lessons that this missing woman, who suffered such a tremendous loss, can teach us about being excellent.

There is something strangely sexual about this book of Esther. Yet we don't want to deal with sex in the church. We like to separate our sexuality from our spirituality. And we like to pretend that sexual politics don't happen in the church. But this biblical record gives us evidence of a woman of excellence who seems to lose her place in history due to blatant sexism. This is also a story about male power being misused. It's a story about a woman with limited options and limited freedom, who did what she had the power to do.

Vashti was the set-up woman for Esther! This is the first lesson we need to learn. A woman of excellence understands that her role in life is to get things set up for the next generation. It ain't all about us. As Christians, our lives are all about the realm of God. And the realm of God is all about community. It's about our being set up by those who came before us. It's about our preparing the way for those yet to follow us.

We learn in Esther 1:11 that the king felt that he had authority over Queen Vashti's sexual self. "Bring the queen, in her Little Kim outfit and let all these boys' tongues lap as they see what I own." Certainly he had the power to call her. He also felt he had the power to display her like an object before a room of drunken men. He thought he was entitled to show her off as his possession, his piece of meat, his private stock, only his honey. That's what he thought.

But lesson number two says that a woman of excellence knows her own boundaries. "Vashti refused to come" (Esth. 1:12). A woman of excellence does not allow others to define her, to establish her limits, or to exploit her sexuality. A woman of excellence is the temple of the Holy Spirit and she's very particular about whom she will permit into her sacred space. She's very clear about the proper time to yield to any other human demand. Women of excellence are led by the Holy Spirit, for they are daughters of the Most High God. Vashti didn't have a wide range of behaviors to select from in her day and age. But she did what she had the power to do. She refused to come.

A woman of excellence will not heed those who bring her messages of exploitation (Esth. 1:10). This is lesson number three. Seven eunuchs were sent to fetch the queen. Seven sexually impotent males, with no vested interest in her well-being, stepped up to her with the degrading message from her spouse. Sista Excellence refused to obey their call.

The media, which exploits the sexuality of women, is a eunuch. The television marketing strategies that tend to portray us primarily as either invisible or drug taking street whores, are eunuchs.

The music industry, when it calls us nasty names and degrading labels, is simply a eunuch. The rap stars who dare to disrespect and disregard us as their mothers, their sisters, their wives, and their daughters, are eunuchs—regardless of how much they grab their empty crotches, perpetrating manhood, imitating virility.

The new genre of movie and television love stories that seek to make us bed hoppers who can't make it without a man and who will do anything for a going-nowhere relationship, is just another jive eunuch.

The government programs that continue to portray us as welfare-seeking, baby-having, man-bashing, never-contributing seekers of free tax dollars, are just more eunuchs.

And the Church, even our own local community church — when it continues to receive women's volunteer services, willing tithes and offerings, choir singing, ushering, Sunday School and Vacation Bible School teaching, pastor's-aid raising, and ministries of missionary service, mother's board, and deaconness while telling women that they have only certain restricted offices and positions that they can hold, and certain proscribed roles that they can play — is the biggest eunuch of all!

When the eunuchs come with messages that disregard our whole contribution, a woman of excellence will refuse even to pay attention! And, by the way, a eunuch can also be another low-down, back-stabbing sister too. Beware of the impotent, regardless of their gender.

Vashti, a woman of excellence, teaches us that we must take ownership of our own sexuality and our own destiny. When she refused to answer the "booty call" of the king, church really began. The deacon board called an emergency meeting (Esth. 1:15): "Now, what shall we do with a rebellious woman? How we gonna act with a woman who dares to set her own agenda? What's up with a sister who doesn't know her place?" And in verse 17: "If the word gets out, all of our women will begin to behave in the same way!"

New laws had to be written. An immediate legislative session was called, for this unprecedented matter of a woman saying "no" had never happened before. There were no rules, no standard operating procedures, no commonly used protocols in place. But a woman of excellence will defy traditions. She will go against convention. She will do the unusual. Her behavior will certainly cause chaos. "We've never done it that way before."

So, to control the situation, to prevent damage to their giant egos and small minds, the boys had the king write Vashti's name out of the history books. Her crown was taken. She was evicted from the royal palace. The designer clothes were snatched. The fine chariot and driver vanished. For Queen Vashti got the royal boot!

In so doing, Vashti set the stage of "next." She went off into a new future. And she opened the door for Queen Esther to come on the scene. In the divine economy of God, every action leads to a grander reaction. A butterfly, hovering over a rose petal in Grand Rapids, Michigan, with the fluttering of her tiny wings, is part of a larger cyclical ecological system that helps to produce a cataclysmic rainstorm in the Andes Mountains a continent away.

Vashti teaches us to stand on our principles. Vashti knew she was a role model. She knew that many other sisters were watching her all the time. "She was entertaining the sistahood in the Queen's Court" (Esth. 1:9). It made no difference that the boys rubbed out her name, for the women were going to spread the news through the grapevine. She was the leader of the pack. She was the queen. The sisters were all watching to see how a diva of excellence would respond to this nasty situation.

Finally, Vashti taught them, me, and you how to do what you have the power to do. For her it was to "just say no!" When a call comes for you to become an object, a thing, and a display—just say no. When a call comes that requires you to let go of your principles, violate your personal ethics, and toss away your integrity—just say no. When a call comes that will disrespect you, take advantage of you, and disrupt your journey to excellence—just say no.

For the real deal is that Vashti becomes the Christ figure in this story. She represents the Living Sacrifice who gave up his royal glory to save the lives of the world. She stands in for the Christ, who refused to bow to the dictates of the temple, who would not adhere to the status quo, who didn't think it was robbery to overthrow the system, uproot the traditions, and mock the old guard.

They told Jesus to stay away from the poor, the marginalized, and the oppressed. Jesus just said no!

They told Jesus not to associate with women, with children, with the ill, and with the dead. Jesus just said no.

They told Jesus to follow the rabbinical laws, to go along to get along, and to join in doing it their way. Jesus just said no.

They said, "Jesus go to the cross. We'll murder you at high noon. We'll pierce you in the side. We'll humiliate you as we rub your name out of the history books. You'll die, Jesus. And then, you will be gone." But Jesus just said no.

He got up. He rose again. He reigns forever. And if you wonder what ever happened to Sista Vashti and you're wondering what's gonna happen to Sista Linda and other bodacious women, just know that every closed eye ain't sleeping and every good-bye ain't gone. For when we learn to say no to the junk of the people, our lives is then in a higher court and we get to move to the next level!

Jesus is our proof that God honors those who have been put out, those who have been cast aside, those who have been dissed, discounted, and devalued. For resurrection is God's eternal "Yes!" to keep us getting on up as we step to excellence, with quickness.

We're yet talking about Vashti. We're yet studying her life and "herstory." Sermons are yet being preached on her. Bible studies and seminary classes continue to list her name and have reports submitted on her bodacious actions. She continues to teach us centuries after the event that led to her banishment! This alone says history did not rub out her name. She's a woman of reknown, a sista of excellence, filled with bodacious womanist wisdom. The girl just did what she had the power to do! That's good enough for each of us!

WOMAN WISDOM SPEAKS: "The simple believe every word, but the wise and prudent consider well their steps" (Prov. 14:15).

WOMANIST WISDOM SAYS: We don't allow ourselves to participate in exploitation. We refuse to sing songs that degrade us. We will not buy the music that exploits us nor allow our children to play it in our homes. We listen carefully to all words of good music before we begin to commit them to our memories and into our spirits. We don't go to movies that don't honor who we are. We don't laugh at jokes that put down other women. For when we are away, we become the joke! We strive to be excellent according to the Bible's standards, not to the rules of society and culture. There is a vast difference between being a godly woman and a feminine fool!

A BODACIOUS WOMAN would know that whatever she does in public is setting a precedent for the next generation. I well remember taking a training course to supervise the housekeeping departments for local hospitals seeking accreditation many years ago when I was young and my knees bent without complaint. My assignment was to clean the public elevator. Being a woman of excellence, I had the inside and outside sparkling. Then I decided to mop and wax the floors. So I hit my knees to spread the wax evenly. This was the way my mother and my grandmother had taught me and modeled for me in their homes. As I backed out of the elevator, on my knees, humming a simple song, there were two housekeepers standing behind me with sour faces. "Who told you to do this?" they asked. After hearing my explanation they said, "Don't ever get on your knees again. For if they see you doing this, they will begin to expect us to do this!" I got the message loud and clear! My role is not to make life more difficult for any sister. Neither is yours!

13

THE BEGGING BOWL

2 Kings 8:1–6

There is no way to dress it up. There is no method of easing the distress. I don't care how many routes you travel to get there, applying for public welfare, public assistance or even disability is humbling, embarrassing, and stressful. Having to come to the place where I have to put in an application for help is a nonverbal message that says I have come to the end of my rope. It says that my resources have been depleted—my ability to do for myself is cut off and all the tricks up my short sleeves have been exhausted.

When I arrive at the place of needing public assistance, I am standing before a hand-out system saying that I can no longer do for myself what is necessary. I need help. I have arrived at the juncture where aid is required. Regardless of how I'm dressed, no matter how much education I have attained, my impressive resume of past academic achievements does not impress the individual who is to receive my application for funds.

My stance, in the front of a desk in this place of provision to the needy, says that my economic well has dried up; my resource bank is depleted and my means of self-support has run out. So I'm there to beg for help. There is no way to fix it up and make it pretty. There is no easing my feelings of distress. Just having to walk in the doors requires, first and foremost, an interior admission of helplessness. My asking for the application demands submission to an ongoing, totally invasive process.

Filling out the multiple forms requires providing information that I don't even talk to my mother about. The evidence required of me demands all sorts of organizational and administrative skill sets that I may not even possess. The inquiries can be demeaning. The waiting process is stress producing as others look me over, trying to figure out my story. The investigation is grueling. And begging for help is always shame producing. For I have come to realize and to admit that I am insufficient on my own. The time has come when I have to beg for help.

To beg is to take low. To beg is to debase oneself. To beg is to humble oneself. To beg is to grovel for one's basic needs. It's not easy to beg. There is no nice way to beg. There is not much pleasure in the act of begging, asking, imploring and beseeching. No one wants to beg. Americans don't like beggars. We are embarrassed by beggars. We are ashamed of beggars. Our ire is raised by beggars. Our indignation is expressed at beggars. For we want to be done with those who have to beg.

Let's bring this up close and personal. When you see someone standing on a corner holding a bowl, what's your first inclination? Most of us will turn our head and act as if we cannot see them. True? If that person is standing directly in your path, holding out a bowl or a hat, how do you respond? If we can't get around the beggar, most of us feel we must respond in some humane fashion. But we may not be not sure how to provide what's necessary to a beggar. Without conscious thought the questions begin to rise in our mind. "What's appropriate?" "How much is enough to give?" "What will this person do with my money?" "Am I simply enabling?" "Am I being scammed?"

Most of the time, without even looking the individual in the eyes, without saying a kind word, without acknowledging that we really do want to be compassionate, we throw some loose change into the bowl and step away as quickly as possible. True? Come on, be honest. What thoughts come to your mind when you see a beggar in the distance?

Whatever negative images come to mind for you, those images are also there in the back of your mind when individuals come to your local congregation seeking mission assistance! Yes! At our pious, upstanding, do-good, faith-based ministries, we have poor attitudes when it comes to those who "beg." We have a serious problem with folks who are not self-sufficient, independent tithers and givers.

As the federal government gives money to states and faith-based projects begin to crop up more frequently, we, the Church of the Living God, have to deal with our attitudes. The names have changed. The rules have been tinkered with so that "we" can control some of the money. We have to face the reality of "welfare reform" that speaks the language of faith-based partnerships and 501c3s instead of the ministry of missions that we know so well.

The Church has joined the secular world and said, "Let's change the way that we talk about "those folks" who have come to ask us for help. Let's see if we can put a new political spin on it, call it by another name and make ourselves feel more comfortable as we attend to their needs with our professional, well-dressed, cultured, and sophisticated selves!" We don't want to own it, it doesn't feel good and doesn't sound nice, but the reality is that the Church is learning how to beg more effectively too!

We continue to watch the news as especially the Catholic Church tries to put a new spin on their handling of all the millions of dollars they have paid out on account of pedophiles in the priesthood. It's affecting their offerings. They are trying various methods to pull in more funds into dwindling coffers. This is called begging! And our annual, well-planned and well-executed stewardship campaigns are only refined methods of begging. So how dare we have difficulty with "those" folks out there?

There is a biblical story that addresses "those folks who beg." It's a story of a very wealthy woman who was kind to a prophet of God. She built him a room in her spacious home and offered him a place of respite, refreshment, and renewal as he traveled his circuit. They became great friends and had a mutual relationship. But a famine came upon the land. The prophet told the woman that she had to leave her vast holdings and go into a foreign land in order to survive.

For more than seven years, this unnamed woman and her family lived among strangers, as aliens, begging in order to survive. When the famine was in her homeland, she and her child came home and entered into the court of the king. They came with begging bowls in their hands. She came to the king to beseech him for welfare. She came to the king seeking assistance, in order to be made whole. She came to the king with an appeal upon her lips for aid. She came into the presence of the king and said, "I ain't too proud to beg!" For she was now a single mother with a child to care for.

Welfare and all of its sister reform acts are of direct concern to women and the children they bear. This story about a woman, her child, and her begging is close to me. For I have been on public welfare. I attended college, on welfare, with two sons to care for. I know the struggle. Been there, done that. Don't need a tee-shirt or cap. The experience is written upon my heart.

What I find amazing in the story is that it reads like this near its conclusion: "The king appointed a worker to her case." This formerly wealthy, upstanding, and prominent woman was reduced to having a caseworker assigned to her. But the end of the story is the best. For the king told the caseworker, "Restore all that was hers. And give her all the proceeds of her fields from the day she left seven years ago until today." This is not some recent and contemporary story, but a biblical story from the ancient text, found in 2 Kings 8:1–6.

So you can see that welfare is a biblical construct that was aimed at the restoration of an individual to a state of wholeness, soundness, health, and emotional well-being. We in America have a twisted concept of providing just enough to those in need to help them get by. As my Granny "usta" say, "They want us to get by on meager fare!"

There are two publications in your local library that require our attention. Both of them were released by Princeton University Press. Both of these books attempt to address the economic plight of America. Both of them seek to deal honestly, forthrightly, and candidly with this pressing issue of welfare reform.

One book, entitled *Work and Welfare,* is written by Robert Solow. Dr. Solow is a Nobel Prize winning economist who directs his attention to how we can get people off welfare and into self-sustaining jobs. Let's not talk about the reality that most "new" jobs pay minimum wage, don't provide medical or dental benefits, and don't allow folks to earn enough money to maintain their own apartments or participate in home ownership. Let's not address the reality that down-sizing, economic restructuring, and the economic spiral downward have all done their part to contribute to the increasing welfare needs of formerly, well-employed, independent people.

Let's not deal with the truth that almost 90 percent of the wealth of the world is in the hands of about 3 percent of the people. Most of the wealth in America can be directly traced back to foreparents who exploited, stole, and enslaved less fortunate folks in order to buy the boots and the shoelaces by which they have now "pulled themselves up." Despite not dealing with all of these truths, Dr. Solow has a ready audience for his book.

The other book, *It Takes a Nation: A New Agenda For Fighting Poverty,* is written from the research of Dr. Rebecca Blank. This is another look at how the "haves" can reduce the number of "have nots" who, their begging bowls in hand, require too much of our hard-earned tax dollars and sheltered monetary gains. The issue so academically addressed by both Dr. Solow and Dr. Blank is a controversy that has even raised its ugly head in the Church.

The question is currently being asked by good churchgoers, "Why is it that our local congregation should provide "welfare" for others who have the same opportunity to pull themselves up and get off their trifling backsides?" Go to the average church and you will find a food pantry or a clothes closet. If there is a food pantry, it normally serves once a week, while we eat three times a day, plus snacks. Be sure to check what the good church folks have donated. You will find much "stuff" that neither they nor their children will have to eat. Don't forget to check out the clothes closet. There you will find junk that the Goodwill would not accept!

We in the church have become Dr. "So-Low" and Dr. "Blank"! "Something must be done about those begging folks. We need funds for our new organ. We need funds for our spoiled, self-indulgent, and selfish youth. We need a family life center for us." In God's Church, there is little compassion for those with their begging bowls in hand. For we are so *low* down as to feel that we are superior. Our minds have gone so *blank*, that we actually have forgotten that each and every one of us is a beggar! We don't have a clue that each and every one of us on the planet earth is on public welfare! Yes! This includes you, too!

The breath we breathe is from the public welfare of our God. The energy that sustains our productivity and intelligence is directly from the public welfare of our God. The food we eat, the harvest we reap, the earth, its seeds and grains that reproduce, all comes from the public welfare of our God. The clothes we wear, the houses we live in, the cars we drive, the church buildings we use, the money we make, the jobs we hold, the stingy portions we try to dole out so niggardly to those in need all come to us by way of God's public welfare. Don't ever get so stuck on stupid, so arrogant and so ignorant that you forget that you too are a beggar with a bowl in your hands!

Let the public welfare of God's generous portion of air cease. Let the waves and electrodes in your brain cease. Let your arms or legs not respond to the transmitters in your brain. Let your tongue cleave to the top of your mouth. Then let's see who has the largest begging bowl.

We can only do whatever small measure of restoring others to wholeness we do with our mission projects and faith-based initiatives because God's welfare plan is working. We can offer our itsy-bitsy outreach to those less fortunate in our communities because the welfare program of a loving God is working. And it works because we have caseworkers assigned to our case.

Thank God for those angels, called our caseworkers, named Goodness and Mercy. These two work overtime to ensure that our begging bowls remain full and that we are not on the other side of the desk, pulpit, or faith-based reception space. Thank God that there is an established cycle to the public welfare reform plan that God has set into motion. It works.

The plan says that God gives to us, right into our begging bowls. Jesus came to make sure that it was "abundant." Then, we are to work with what is put into our bowl and make every attempt to use the gifts and talents we have to increase it. Finally, we are to share from our bowls with others, remembering who filled our bowl in the first place. Tithing 10 percent of our monetary gain is God's repayment plan! As we give from our begging bowls, God replenishes. This is called the law of sowing and reaping. And God wills that restoration, wholeness, and health is our portion. "Beloved, I wish above all things that you prosper and be in good health even as your soul prospers" (3 John 2).

My sisters, not one of us is too good to cooperate with God's welfare plan for the benefit of all humanity. This is a marvelous invitation for us to help our local mission group or faith-based ministry to reevaluate how we're addressing the needs in our communities. For we are dependent upon God and interdependent upon each other. Yes! Even those of us who dare to wear designer clothes, have attained pompous titles, have earned degrees, and possess a posturing attitude are welfare recipients. And I thank God that those caseworkers have been assigned to our case and we have received so many multiple benefits that others felt we didn't need or deserve!

There is no question. There is no debate. We cannot take a compromise position with all the benefits sitting in our begging bowls. We must willingly, cheerfully, and enthusiastically work with God to envision, strategize, and offer our begging bowls to others. It is the very least that we can do. Establishing faith-based partnerships, volunteering, networking, and being community for each other is the way God designed the world. Whatever we offer is simply our reasonable portion of service and gratitude to the Awesome Mystery whom we call God.

Public welfare is our God-given legacy. Passing it on is our gift to God in return. The day of accountability is at hand. Those who come looking for help from us have another caseworker assigned to their case. God has called me and you to be their caseworkers for help, restoration, and wholeness. It's God's truth!

WOMAN WISDOM SPEAKS: "Those who oppress the poor reproach the Creator. Those who honor God have mercy on those in need" (Prov. 14:31).

WOMANIST WISDOM SAYS: The local church has always been in the forefront of meeting needs in our community. Most historical black colleges were started in the basements of local churches. It is yet common to find tutoring programs, computer classes, parenting classes, and even financial information within the curriculum of the local church's Christian Education programs. And, whatever the immediate need, there are folks available to round them up and help them to "see" the vision too. Repeat complaints often offer guidance to specific needs! Listen closely to what is not being said.

A BODACIOUS WOMAN would call together five or six sisters for tea-cakes and imported tea served out of Mama's silver teapot and ask them what they have noticed missing in the community. She would allow them to talk her into doing something that they would be glad to help do!

14

BROKEN BOUNDARIES

Judges 19

*S*he was like a lamb before its slaughterers. She never spoke a word that anyone remembered, although I'm sure that she had cried aloud for help. She had to have screamed out in pain. She must have wept and wailed in anguish. She must have screeched something terrible. But, like the slaughterers before the lamb, no one recorded her words. They didn't want to hear her words. They refused to acknowledge her calls, her cries, her sighs. Her wails didn't stop her slaughter. Her tears didn't stench the blood flow. Even her last breath was unrecorded, if indeed she dared to mouth a last word.

For they all say, "It didn't hurt her." They all say, "She liked it." They all say, "She wanted it." They all say, "She didn't say 'no.'" They all say, "Sure she resisted, it's more fun that way." They all say, "She should have said something if she didn't want it." While her cries, her screams, her moans, her groans, her pain, her hurt, and her anguish went unheeded by a vicious, violent mob, heaven heard every moan. Her blood cried out a resounding testimony of terror against women. And the stones in an ancient chorus mourned her unheard screams. Mother Earth received another daughter and held her closely as she silently died.[1]

Once upon a time, a singing preacher dismembered his wife. The Church split and went to war because of it. Once upon a time, a singing preacher dismembered his wife. This was the ultimate act of domestic violence. And the Church acts as if it never happened. Once upon a time, a singing preacher hacked his wife into twelve pieces after allowing her to be gang raped, physically violated, and sexually abused all night long. Her name is never mentioned. Her story is seldom told. Her voice was hushed in the pages of the biblical canon. But today it is her blood that cries out about our broken boundaries in the Church!

Did our sister ask for rape because she was female? Perhaps it was due to her provocative dress that the rape was perpetrated. Or could it have been that all women want to be handled in a rough manner? Maybe it was simply what she deserved for being in the wrong place at the right time. I wonder if she was firm in her statement that she did not desire to be involved in this sexual act with a group of men? Do you think anyone would have heard her when she yelled, screamed, and shouted out a loud, "No!"?

Was there anyone there to advocate for her as a victim of a senseless crime of sexual violence? Were there any press conferences called, bureaucratic investigations required, or legislation passed to prevent this violation of her personal boundaries from ever happening again in the Church? Or is the continuing silence of the Church another one of the great impasses that we rarely dare to mention in "open company"?

Her death was not the end of the story. For the story continues to be repeated in your church and mine. We live in a continuing cycle of violence against women. Our grandmothers felt the pain. Our mothers felt the pain. We—contemporary, sophisticated, seminary trained, professional women—feel the same pain. And our daughters and our granddaughters will feel the pain until we decide to break the silence. For the pain of broken boundaries is part of our heritage as women in the church. Is it any wonder that we—who have been trained to pleasure men, to feed men, to clothe men, to birth men—will get just as silent when we discover another woman whose been beaten, misused, raped, and then hacked to pieces and set out on public display?

The blood of this, our biblical sister, gives us a strong voice to hear. Her witness, her testimony, and her story provide the context for the unnamed, painful shame that the Church harbors, hides, seals, and validates as acceptable behavior. We must uncover this sister's story as it is told in Judges, chapter 19. The recollection of a ghastly chain of events leading to this text of terror begins with the warning: "In those days Israel had no king."

No king meant that there was no moral representative of the Most High God alive, and active on behalf of the Creator. No king meant that there was no value placed upon the life, the rights and the privileges of the last, the least, and the neglected, whether woman, child, or foreigner. No king meant there was no political figure to maintain, establish, or set forth the Sovereign's guidelines for relationships—of either the Church or the state. No king meant that every tub sat on its own bottom, did its own thing, called its own shots—and God bless the child who had "his" own! No king meant that all boundaries were fluid, flexible, and movable at human will. "In those days Israel had no king." This meant that the voice, the will, and the divine rule of God was absent from the Church.

A Levite, a member of the singing house of Israel's priestly line, took a concubine for a wife. Notice the term used is "wife." Because of her unfaithfulness to him, she returned to her father's house. After four months without her, the Levite, her husband, took along his servant and two donkeys as he went to persuade her to come home. She agreed to go back to his home as his wife.

As they were making the return trip home, they stopped in territory that was occupied by the tribe of Benjamin. An old man of the tribe took pity on the group of travelers and invited them to come and spend the night in his home. He offered them his hospitality and provided the Levite with plenty of refreshment. While the men were enjoying each other's company, "some wicked men from the city surrounded the house," demanding to have sex with the "new man" in town!

To prevent a violation of his hospitality, the old man offered the men of his town both his virgin daughter and the Levite's wife! The words he used were these: "I will bring them out to you now, and you can use them and do to them whatever you wish. But to this man don't do such a disgraceful thing" (Judg. 19:23–24). The men of the city would not listen to him. "So the Levite took his concubine" (notice the term concubine now!) "and sent her outside to them. And they raped her and abused her throughout the night and at dawn they let her go. At daybreak the woman went back to the house where her master" (insert the word husband) "was staying, fell down at the door, and lay there until morning" (Judg. 19:25–26).

"When her master" (insert the word husband) "got up in the morning and opened the door of the house and stepped out to continue on his way, there lay the concubine, fallen in the doorway of the house with her hands on the threshold. He said to her, 'Get up; let's go.' But there was no answer. Then the man put her on his donkey and set out for home. When he reached home, he took a knife and cut up his concubine" (insert the word wife) "limb by limb, into twelve mangled parts and sent them into all the areas of Israel. Everyone who saw it said, 'Such a thing has never been seen or done, not since the day Israel came up out of Egypt.' Think about it! Consider it! Tell us what to do!'" The chapter ends at verses 27–30.

The Levite represents the Church! The woman represents every female in the Church! Actually, she is the Christ figure in the story! She is the foremothers. She is our mother. She is us! And unless we act in concert to address this issue, forthrightly and directly, she is our daughters! For women have inherited this role of concubine, the second-class wife, who is easily able to become the sacrificial lamb.

The old man represents the men in the life of the Church who are not worthy of us! He is everyone of those who don't deserve us. He is each male who is ready and willing to deny our humanity while living off our multiple and various personal sacrifices.

The gang rapers represent the Church culture that continues to consider women as dispensable objects and servants. However, the Bible calls us to "Think about it! Consider it! Tell us what to do!" This passage is a call for us to break the silence and begin the authentic work of dealing with the necessary changes that will bring healing to the violated boundaries among us.

The Word of God tells the truth about the whole people of God. This passage is called a text of terror by theologian Phyllis Tribble. For this passage is filled with explicit violence, vile shock, horrible pain, and deviant sexual assault. This passage calls our attention to the fact that as the woman/wife/concubine came to the house where the Levite had slept well, after putting her out to be used and mis-used all night, she put her hand, in supplication for help, on the threshold of the door to the house.

There is great symbolism implied in this act. For she was the woman/wife/concubine of the priest. In the text we move back and forth between her exact role in his life. However, one thing is per-fectly clear: the priest had responsibility for her well-being. The priest went to get her. The priest brought her along with him to return to his dwelling place. And she, this woman, our sister, anticipated, ex-pected, and was looking for protection, assistance, care, and comfort after a malicious and violent attack on her personhood. If you can't go to the Church for help when you have been raped by the world, where can you go? This question begs for our consideration.

We must also be clear about the fact that the "wicked men" were not foreigners. These evil men were not despised gentiles. Nor were these rapists the despicable, ungodly, lowlife heathens. These men who commit this act of gang rape were Jews, well acquainted with the God of Israel. These were Jewish men especially chosen by God to be lights to the foreign, gentile, and heathen world! These were Jewish men who attended tabernacle ritual, participated in taber-nacle worship, and had been circumcised to indicate their special status with God!

These "great" patriarchs of our present Church came to involve themselves in homosexual relationships with the "fresh new male meat" in their town! When the old man would not violate the codes of hospitality, these great churchmen did not hesitate to deliberately abuse, rape, and murder an innocent woman, who was their sister in the Jewish community. She was someone's Jewish daughter. She was someone's Jewish wife. She may have been someone's Jewish sister, cousin, or aunt. She was a female member of "their" nation.

If it was just one story, perhaps we could act surprised that we discover this type of brutal behavior against women in Scripture.

However, this story is linked to Adam's finger of blame at Eve. This story is linked to Lot and the men of Sodom and Gomorrah. This story is linked to Sarah and Abraham's abusive treatment of Haggar. This story is linked to the rubbing out of the historical record of Vashti when she refused to be a public display object for the king, while Esther was pimped by Mordacai to pass in order to win her place in the palace. This story is linked to a woman who met Jesus at the well after being set aside by five husbands in the Church and left with a hole in her soul. This story is linked to a woman that Jesus delivered from seven demons, all of which the Church wants to name as sexual. This story is linked to a woman who was "caught in adultery," while the common name for sex alone is masturbation! This story is simply part of a series of continuing stories that form patterns evidencing mistreatment of women in the Church.

What is painful, disappointing, and harmful is the fact that we, the women in the Church, seem to find it acceptable. "We" is certainly an inclusive word. For women, as a whole, don't want to address the painful sexual issues in the Church either. "We" have all tried in various and sundry ways to erase, vanquish, and delete the shameful manner in which women are exploited day by day. "We" collude in the silence. "We" hurt ourselves. And "we" hurt each other with our silence!

We are at war in the Church! You and I are challenged, compelled, and mandated to "Think about it! Consider it! And, tell the Church what to do!" For me, the initial step is for us to break through the boundaries of silence. For me, the next step is to be cognizant of the reality that over one-half of our local congregations have texts of terror written into the personal chapters of their lives. And for me the final step is to begin the covenant process of telling our stories, calling our members to share in their stories, naming the perpetrators, and giving voice to the cry of our sister's spilled blood.

As a woman with a personal investment in this story, I have struggled to find the good news in this text. As a woman challenged to preach and to teach the good news of Jesus to a hurting and pain-filled Church, I have wrestled with the issues of "where was God" in this story? As a sister who knows intimately the details of having been raped by the Church, and yet having my hands on the threshold of the door to the Church, I have grappled with how to make peace with a God who was silent.

As I approached another Palm Sunday, I felt some resolution in my spirit. For the Palm Sunday parade, which precedes the Easter Sunday celebration, outlines the story of preparation by Jesus and Da Boys. I didn't find it told in the story of the evangelist John. I couldn't find it in the story recorded by the evangelist Luke. Even Mark, the oldest recorded Gospel, did not have my answer. But in the story outlined by Matthew for the Jewish Church, I found these words in chapter 21, verse 1. "And Jesus sent two disciples, saying to them, 'Go into the village . . . immediately you will find a donkey tied, and a colt with her. Loose them and bring them to me. And if anyone says anything to you, you shall say, "The Lord has need of them" and immediately he will send them.'"

The first question that comes to mind when I read this very familiar passage of scripture is "Why did Jesus need both of the animals?" We don't read anywhere that he rode them both. We don't have any indication that one of the disciples was chosen to ride along with him. We don't see in any of the stories where someone from the crowd was invited to get aboard and act like they belonged with the Jesus crowd of admirers. It's after deliberating over these issues that I am reminded that the body of the hacked-up woman was thrown across the back of a donkey!

Jesus declared that he had been sent to the household of Israel. This included that awful, uncaring priest, the old inhospitable man, those sex-crazed brothers, and the good-for-nothing servant of the priest, from whom we never hear anything in the text. Jesus came to gather up all the pieces of broken women and put them back together again! I am free to believe that the colt was to represent that women and their children were symbolically riding with Jesus that day. For the grand Palm Sunday parade indicated that there was now a King in Israel! For me and for "we" this is awesome and bodacious news! Think about it! Consider it! Then, run and tell that!

WOMAN WISDOM SPEAKS: "The name of the Lord is a strong tower; the righteous run to it and are safe" (Prov. 17:10).

WOMANIST WISDOM SAYS: The days of silence in the Church are over! The Catholic Church is reeling from the stories of sexual abuse committed over the years by parish priests. The Catholic Church has paid out multimillions of dollars to squash the news, deny the charges, and keep the public from finding out that the sexual boundaries have been broken repeatedly over the years. The Church now has to deal with the sin within! "We" are the Church. "We" have been abused. "We" need to call together the sisterhood and allow the truth to be told, the perpetrators named, and the charges filed so that "we" might be free to live the abundant life that Jesus died for us to obtain.

A BODACIOUS WOMAN would shout her truth from the rooftops! She would write it in a book! She would go on the radio and television and to the printed media and allow the world to know that she is a worthwhile woman with her hands on the threshold of the doors of the Church. Then she would demand that the Church doors open to recognize and receive her fully. She would gather the resources of her city, including the shelters, abuse hotlines, domestic violence advocates, and those charged with the responsibility of making safe places for women and their children, and she would call together a forum where the voices might be a strong and noisy collective, too loud to be ignored or dismissed!

15

LEGACY

Proverbs 31

"Come on, follow me." Fourth period is English Lit. Through the auditorium, backstage, up three flights of circular stairs and to the classroom on the left side of the narrow corridor. Find a seat, catch your breath, and get ready for a great time of reading and discussing adventure. Mrs. House is so cool. She's a sharp dresser. Look at that makeup and hair style. She's fun to be with, never puts us down because we're inhospitable—we're kids. She makes learning so exciting. Listen to how she talks. I have never heard her raise her voice at any kid. And you know we can really cut up and act crazy. But she always speaks real low and has respect for us. She finds books that are good for us, and they make sense. Some of them are even interesting. Goodness, I've talked so much until the period is over. "Naw, you go ahead. I'm going to stay behind and talk to Mrs. House."

That was seventh grade and I can remember it as freshly as if it were yesterday. It was never too hot, too cold, or too far to climb all those stairs to get to Mrs. House. It really wasn't her English Lit class that I was so crazy about. It was this woman who always had time for me. Talk about being "touched by an angel"; I had that experience years ago.

My life was not going well. I was being sexually abused by my father, a pastor. There was no one I could tell. I just wanted my Mama to see what was going on right before her eyes. I was always nervous, skittery, and jumpy. Why didn't she understand that something was wrong? I couldn't talk to anyone at church. I couldn't tell any of my friends. It was too shameful to even think about. It was way too early for "just say no" programs. Oprah Winfrey was having her own personal difficulties and didn't have even a radio show! My options were extremely limited. But Hortense House noticed me!

One day, she asked me to remain after class. "Linda, do you want to talk?" What an open invitation. She began to stay in her classroom for lunch hour so that we could just sit and talk. Sometimes I would just sit and cry. I never told her my real home story. She just knew something was not right in my life. Her two nephews were my neighbors, Marvin and Roy. Her sister and my mother were in the same women's organizations. We lived in a close-knit community. I was one of the neighborhood children and she took time for me. Today, I realize that Hortense was a very young woman during that period; she had a young son and was trying to get readjusted after a divorce. She needed her own space, and yet she allowed me to intrude into her time and her life.

Money was scarce in our home and most of the time I had to walk home to eat lunch. So, at least two days a week, Mrs. House would ask me to go the cafeteria and bring her back lunch. "And while you're there, why not get one for yourself?" I remember those lunches. She was so refined; she made a desktop a special serving station and used plastic cutlery with decorum. She taught me how to "dine out." Then, she invited me to meet her one Saturday at the Copper Kettle, downtown. I had never been there. This had been a formerly "all Anglo" establishment, where folks like us could not enter. But civil rights came into the picture, barriers came down, and we went to have high tea. I had never seen so much silverware in one place (my place setting!) at one time. So I watched Mrs. House and imitated her style. I will always remember the pride I felt sitting there with her, my teacher, my friend. Of course she treated! This was my formal, initial introduction into a very different culture. I'll never forget it!

Then there was the Ebony Fashion Fair. Only the "upper crust" could afford to attend "the" cultural affair in our community. When the Fair came to town, everybody who was anybody was in attendance. None of the folks I knew would ever be there; it was a scholarship fund raiser, and the ticket prices were out of their league. But Mrs. House stopped by my home one evening. She asked my mother if she could take me to see the fashion show. There is no way I can describe my elation. I was going to an event that none of my peers had ever attended. I was going with a teacher who was willing to let the whole world know she felt that I was "special."

The Copper Kettle and the Fashion Fair stand out for me as two landmark events in the establishment of my womanhood. Hortense provided adventures that my mother could not. Hortense gave me a sense of ethnic pride in the achievements of my culture. Hortense led me into a search for "fine things," which continues today. She was a first-rate teacher. For she not only taught with the written and spoken word, she was a living example for my adult life. She put ideas of grandeur into my head about a future my parents could not even imagine. She "saw" a twinkle inside of me that she was determined to "rub" into a bright star.

Mrs. House and I had a relationship that was to last. Every setback in school, I talked over with her. Every boyfriend, I presented for her approval. Every achievement I celebrated with her. Every funny incident, I shared with her. The pain of my home life was made easier to bear because of her availability to me throughout those formative years. She did it because she was called by the Creator to teach. Teaching was not a job for her. Teaching was not just a career path. Teaching was not simply a role she played from eight until three-thirty. She was a master teacher. Her whole self was involved in teaching lessons that last a lifetime.

Because of her role in my life, I became a teacher. Because of her mentoring, today I am a pastor-teacher. I want, more than anything else, to help others discover a future they don't realize they can have. My active involvement in ministry to women is due to the grand legacy I received in an upstairs classroom, backstage of the auditorium, with an English Lit instructor. Hortense has helped me to de-

velop that "inner eye" into the pained spirits of my sisters. I see and
hear with my heart, not with my eyes. She gave that insight to me.

Today I have one biological daughter, Grian Eunyke. I have five
adopted daughters, in different parts of the country—Angie, Tracy,
Jacqui, Darlene, and Sandi. I am "Reverend Mother" to these five. I
was drawn to the "neglected little girl" who lived within each of them.
They were drawn to my care and nurture. They receive from me the
many benefits I gained in my backstage "upper room." Our sharing is
always honest, authentic and open. My life is an open book with them.
They know of my struggles and my celebrations. I have not hidden my
past from them, but have been able to share it because Mrs. House
brought hope to what could have been a very hopeless situation.

In Holy Scriptures, the "upper room" is that place where the disciples of Jesus Christ were filled with the Spirit of God. In community, they were given the power to do effective, life-changing ministry to all the world. I have "been there!" I live my life to "do that!"
Mrs. House is yet in my life, a mentor, a guide, a mother-figure, and
a continuing friend. Her house is one of those places I have to stop
by whenever I'm back home. She stands tall in my mind as I write
every line in my books for women. She consistently urges me to "tell
the story." Without her input and involvement in my life, I don't
know where I would be today. My world is larger and more ex-
panded because of her. As she has walked through grief in recent
years, I have had the joy of being there for her, in the circle of her
many friends. I was often her early morning wake-up call and many
times her late night check-up call. For she is important to me. She
is my living legacy. I love her dearly.

Hortense has retired now. She is raising a granddaughter and
continuing to instill values that will last into future generations. She
continues to volunteer as counselor to young women and works
faithfully with her Delta Sorority sisters. Her teaching continues and
the world is made better. Some would say it was fate that put me in
her class in the seventh grade. I believe it was an act of the Divine.
For God knew that my life needed a healing balm, a gentle touch
and a sweetness that home could not supply. But "today" was in my
future and Hortense House helped me to see myself in it. Then she
took me by my hand and said, "Linda, I will show you the way."

"What did you say, Ms. House? I'm sorry. I was sitting here day-dreaming!"

WOMAN WISDOM SPEAKS: "Many daughters have done well, but you surpass them all. Charm is deceitful and beauty is passing, but a woman who reverences God shall be praised. Give her of the fruit of her hands, and let her own works praise her in the gates" (Prov. 31:29–31).

WOMANIST WISDOM SAYS: We are all to leave a legacy invested within the life of another female! We were created to make a difference in this world. Lights only have one purpose and that is to light up the world around them. I'm thankful for having seen a great light in Mrs. House. I pray mine shines as well.

A BODACIOUS WOMAN has wanted to end this time with you honoring the woman who reached out her hand to me in the seventh grade and prevented me from becoming stagnant in life. Hortense showed me a different world. Hortense made me know that I was valuable and worthwhile. Hortense role modeled a bodacious woman for me . . . now don't blame her for how far I have taken her lead! But I honor the woman she was and the great woman she continues to be in all the world that she impacts.

When the Bible asks the question, "Who can find a woman of virtue?" as it does in the last chapter of Proverbs, I have a ready answer. It's Hortense House. When the Word declares that her value is worth more than jewels, I can testify that this is true of Hortense. I am only one of her "living testimonies"! She is a teacher par excellence and I'm so very thankful she taught me how to read and write well enough to be able to share with you, my sisters.

16

THE AFTERWORD

(Wisdom Is a Girl Named Mulan!)

*E*very wise woman should own a copy of the video entitled *Mulan*. We had to take Giraurd to see the Disney release when it first came out. I sat down prepared to eat my popcorn and take a quick snooze, until I heard the voice of the "wannabe dragon," who sounded suspiciously like Eddie Murphy. Did I ever wake up! The movie tells the story of a young Chinese girl who wants to be loyal to her family traditions, get married, have a child, and be a "good wife" to the man selected by the marriage maker. But the best laid plans go astray.

When the emperor decrees that a man from each family must serve in the Imperial Army to fight off the invasion led by a mighty Hun warrior, her crippled father must return to active duty. Although Mulan knows the consequences (death!) of impersonating an officer for any reason, she decides to enter the army in her father's place. She prays before the ancestral altar, and Mushu, the "wannabe," is dispatched as a guardian spirit to provide wisdom.

Mulan goes off to war. The story is wonderful. The story should be seen by every young woman in America, especially those of color. This is a movie that teaches lessons of courage, honor, and love. And the heroine is a young woman — Mulan. It turns out the she is wiser than Mushu (although the boy is hugely funny!).

The young woman is not a Christian. Yet, in her tradition she shows others the power of family love; she instills in them honor and respect for the elders, and she shows them how to seek the guidance of Wisdom in every endeavor. She is part of a wonderful family, although she is an only child and a girl. She is a rebel spirit and her father loves her in spite of her nonconforming ways. For she does not please the matchmaker who personifies tradition and the Chinese way. Her grandmother, who lives with them, is a stitch with her witty and uncensored remarks. She illustrates the point that "Wisdom is more precious than rubies, and nothing you desire can compare with her" (Prov. 8:11).

Many might feel that Mulan is foolish in risking her life by impersonating a man and entering the army Many might conclude that she put the lives of worthy men at risk when she could not measure up to their physical strength. But Womanist Wisdom provided her with wise ways to get around her lack of "manly strength." For what macho brawn cannot do, the Womanist Wisdom of the Ancient of Days teaches her to accomplish. This is the same Womanist Wisdom that led Harriet Tubman to lead slaves to freedom as a female Moses. It was this same Womanist Wisdom that called Isabella Bumpry to change her name to Sojourner Truth and demand the right to vote for people of color. This is the same Womanist Wisdom that led Mary McCloud Bethune to begin an educational institution on a garbage dump and Mary Church Terrill to enlist the powers that be to begin the NAACP. Womanist Wisdom has led many women to do the seemingly insane and win despite their femaleness. And Womanist Wisdom ain't through yet!

I write in the month of March. It's my birth month as well as International Woman's History Month. March 8 is International Woman's History Day. There are not enough womanist groups calling together celebrations! And it concerns me as I am called to join with other groups in recognition of this grand occasion. As many collectives of women's organizations continue to also celebrate women's right to vote and to uplift the name of Susan B. Anthony, I want us to recall the truth of that convention held in Ohio.

Remember that Sister Susan was not concerned with attaining the vote for African slaves. She agreed with the contemporary thought of her day, that Africans were not fully human. Remember that the Constitution of this country counted each slave as only three-fifths of a person! Don't forget your history!

It took the Womanist Wisdom of Sister Sojourner Truth, whose name was changed by God, to carry the message of slaves to the forefront of our Anglo sister's thought-life. She dared to raise the question, "And ain't I a woman?" She dared to remind the nation that God made us all—black, brown, white, red, yellow, and green (with envy!). All of us were created by God. Some of us are yet "wannabes!" But thank God that Woman Wisdom will work in spite of our arrogance and ignorance!

The call of this woman named Wisdom continues to ring aloud throughout the world. She yet runs the streets looking for those who will heed her counsel. "Listen, for I have worthy things to say; I open my lips to speak what is right" (Prov. 8:6). I agree with my Anglo sisters that we all need to be a living legacy for the world to see and to imitate. Womanist Wisdom calls me to also remember the truth of my history and not be deceived into believing or celebrating half truths!

Today I celebrate the Womanist Wisdom found in a little girl of color named Mulan. I thank God for the woman who demanded the right to the vote for me. Her name is Sojourner Truth, not Susan B. Anthony!

I invite you to always heed the voice of this woman called Wisdom. She's yet offering wise counsel. She continues to help us remember our divine potential. She continues to open our eyes to unique and different methods to make ways where there is not even a path or trail. She continues to help us imagine the new and the never was before. She continues to point the way to our better and grander future. Walk on with faith in God. Move ahead with hope in Jesus Christ. Be empowered by the fire of the Holy Spirit. And engage often the counsel of Woman Wisdom. Know that with this creative circle of cheerleaders, you do have it going on! You are all that and a big bag of chips! Don't listen to anything different. And don't forget to exploit your specialness as you sashay your way into more wise, less dramatic tomorrows!

Girlfriends, thanks for spending these precious hours with me. Thanks for taking seriously the words of the Scriptures that God prepared to help us grow into our divine destiny. Thanks for reading slowly, and rereading, so that your light will shine more brightly in the days to come. For God called us to be bodacious. God made wisdom available for us. God wants us to twinkle, twinkle as the great stars that we are! Get your twinkle on, Girlfriend. God's got your back. Jesus rose so that you could twinkle too. The Holy Spirit will provide you the power to move ahead. The angels are cheering you. And I'm praying your strength and good success in our Bodacious God! Shalom! God's best shalom . . . 'til we meet the next time in pages like these. Twinkle!

Let's pray together:

God of technicolored people and God called by many assorted names, we approach your throne of grace at your invitation. We come boldly, for you have promised us grace and mercy to help us in our time of need. Good God, we need you now! Amazing God, you continue to challenge us and to call us to move on up a little higher. It scares us. It makes us nervous. We've become comfortable right where we are. We bless you for the journey so far. We can look back over our lives and see how you have already brought us from a mighty long way.

We have taken giant steps. We have fallen and been hurt. We have bruises, scrapes, and scars to cover our hands and knees, and there are too many written on the schematic of our hearts! We dared to read the stories of bodacious wise women, but every story is about struggle, wrestling, and change. Isn't there an easier way to become bodacious? Can't the wisdom we need find us, overtake us, and teach us without pain? We really don't want to hurt.

What do you mean that Jesus learned obedience through the things that he suffered? What are you talking about when you say that each one of us must go through the fire of afflictions? Haven't I had enough? I feel strong enough already!

Oh, you're saying that Wisdom is not about strength? Wisdom is about being closer to you? Wisdom is about being stamped with your stamp of "Woman of Worth and Value?" Wisdom is about making you look good in the world? Well, I did sign up for this graduate course. I've read the offered text. Now it's time for the next test? Already? I'm not quite prepared. Oh, that's what Woman Wisdom is all about? Well, the world needs to be on the alert, for it seems as if another bodacious wise woman has been called and is being created!

Thanks for believing that I can be of use to you. Thanks for providing all that I will need. And thanks for the comfort of bodacious womanist cheerleaders all around. Thanks for unveiling yourself to me again, through the lives and service of the "sistahood!"

I'm covered by the blood of Jesus. I'm the righteous of yours. And I have the right to call you whenever, wherever, and however I need. HELP! NOW! In the name of Jesus Christ I pray. It is so now and forevermore! Thanks be to God!

ENDNOTES

Preface

1. Katie Cannon, *Black Womanist Ethics* (New York: Scholars Press, 1988), 31.

2. Frances Beal, "Slave of a Slave No More," *The Black Scholar* 12 (Nov.–Dec. 1981), 16–17.

3. Jacquelyn Grant, *White Women's Christ and Black Women's Jesus* (New York: Scholars Press, 1989), 199.

4 .Ibid, 210.

5. Martin Luther King Jr., *Where Do We Go From Here? Chaos or Community* (New York: Harper & Row, 1968), 89.

Chapter 5

1. Sam Cooke, "A Change Is Gonna Come" © 1963 ABKO Music LTD/MCA Music LTD.

Chapter 6

1. Dorothy Norwood and Alvin Darling (lyrics and music), "Victory Is Mine," arranged by Stephen Kay © 2000 GIA Publications, Chicago. Used with permission in the GIA *African American Heritage Hymnal*, 489.

Chapter 7

1. Alfred H. Ackley, "He Lives" © 1933, renewed 1961 The Rodehaver Co.

Chapter 10

1. Richard Blanchard, "Fill My Cup, Lord" © 1959 by Richard Blanchard, assigned to Sacred Songs. © 1964 Sacred Songs.

Chapter 14

1. Michael Williams, ed., *The Storyteller's Companion to the Bible: Old Testament Women* (Nashville: Abington Press, 1993), 108.

OTHER BOOKS FROM THE PILGRIM PRESS

JESUS AND THOSE BODACIOUS WOMEN
Life Lessons from One Sister to Another
LINDA H. HOLLIES

0-8298-1246-6/paper/224 pages/$11.95

Linda Hollies serves up new spins on the stories of biblical women.
From Eve to Mary Magdalene, portraits of the bodaciousness of the many
matriarchs of the Christian tradition will prove to be blessings for readers.
Study questions and suggestions providing examples of how to grow in
faith and spirituality, and courage are included at the end of each chapter.

TAKING BACK MY YESTERDAYS
Lessons in Forgiving and Moving Forward with Your Life
LINDA H. HOLLIES

0-8298-1208-3/paper/192 pages/$10.95

"A must read book! Linda Hollies has successfully combined personal
honesty and solid biblical storytelling to teach us how to forgive and let
go of yesterday. . . . The prayers will inspire you. The principles will
encourage you. The psalms will direct your path." Iyanla Vanzant, author
Acts of Faith, talk show host of IYANLA.

To order these or any other books from The Pilgrim Press call or write to:

THE PILGRIM PRESS
700 PROSPECT AVENUE EAST
CLEVELAND, OHIO 44115-1100

PHONE ORDERS: 1-800-537-3394 (M–F, 8:30 AM–4:30 PM ET)
FAX ORDERS: 216-736-2206

Please include shipping charges of $4.00 for the first book and
$0.75 for each additional book.

Or order from our web site at www.pilgrimpress.com.
Prices subject to change without notice.